The Diary of an Isle Royale School Teacher

Dorothy Peterman Simonson

Isle Royale Natural History Association
Houghton, Michigan 49931

Publication of this edition was made possible by a generous gift from Joyce and John VanWestenburg of Chassell, MI, for whom Isle Royale is a very special place.

Cover Photo:
Dorothy and Bob Simonson.
--Robert Simonson Collection.

Fourth Printing, May, 2004

Printed in U.S.A.
Book Concern Printers, Hancock, MI 49930
Copyright © by The Isle Royale
Natural History Association

ISBN 0-935289-02-X

Dorothy Simonson's original handwritten diary is in the Michigan Technological University Archives and Copper Country Historical Collections of the J. Robert Van Pelt Library, Houghton, Michigan. This published version was made possible through the typing effort of Diane Held who copied it into a Macintosh computer, and Kathy Weber who volunteered to provide the bracketed notations so that readers might better comprehend the people, places and things mentioned by Dorothy. Many thanks also to numerous readers who assured the accuracy of these transcriptions including Gayle Pekkala, Ellen Croll, H. Irene Kokko, Alma Pekkala, Bob Linn, Sharon Ringler, Bonee Bonini, Clarice Karry and Tim Gardner.

Bruce Weber
Project Editor

Foreword

My mother had always wanted to publish this journal. After we left the Island, however, she had her hands full trying to raise a son and pound a little knowledge into his head — not an easy task. She also was pursuing her own education, and trying to keep the wolf from the door. She always insisted the journal would not be published until she could edit some of the more personal comments. Well, *"tempus fugit"* and it never got done. She assigned me the task of publishing the journal, if I so desired, but with instructions to do the necessary editing. I usually followed her orders, and generally got into trouble when I didn't. After re-reading her words, however, I felt I could change very little except for punctuation and spelling. I feel that the swings of emotion, the ups and downs of spirit, and the sometimes intemperate personal remarks recorded, give this diary the reality of Isle Royale as it was then — wonderous, awe inspiring, beautiful and majestic; but countered by the isolation, the sometimes claustrophobic atmosphere, the weariness, the immensity of the task, the very real hardships. The words that follow record the true feelings and unabridged thoughts of a dedicated teacher, a wonderful mother, and a great friend.

Bob Simonson

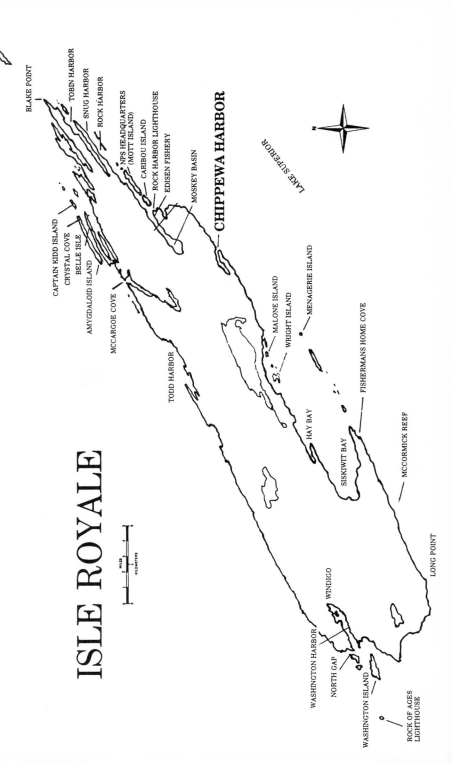

ISLE ROYALE

BLAKE POINT
TOBIN HARBOR
SNUG HARBOR
ROCK HARBOR
NPS HEADQUARTERS (MOTT ISLAND)
CARIBOU ISLAND
ROCK HARBOR LIGHTHOUSE
EDISEN FISHERY
MOSKEY BASIN
CHIPPEWA HARBOR
CAPTAIN KIDD ISLAND
CRYSTAL COVE
BELLE ISLE
AMYGDALOID ISLAND
MCCARGOE COVE
TODD HARBOR
MALONE ISLAND
WRIGHT ISLAND
MENAGERIE ISLAND
FISHERMANS HOME COVE
HAY BAY
SISKIWIT BAY
MCCORMICK REEF
WINDIGO
WASHINGTON HARBOR
NORTH GAP
WASHINGTON ISLAND
ROCK OF AGES LIGHTHOUSE
LONG POINT

LAKE SUPERIOR

N

MILES
KILOMETERS

September 13, 1932

Bob and I left Duluth at 10:30 A.M. on the S.S. "Winyah," a fish-mail boat which runs between Isle Royale and Duluth. It was a cold, gray morning and I felt a sinking sensation in the pit of my stomach as we pulled away from the dock and waved goodbye to Mama and Gretchen [Gretchen Ashley, Dorothy's sister] who had driven us to Duluth the day before. But the sun came out before long and as we plowed northeast through a heavy rolling sea, our spirits rose and we prepared to enjoy our trip. We passed Two Harbors at 12:30 P.M. — then went down to lunch, which was very good, served in the kitchen in close proximity to the stove on one side and the cook's bunk on the other. The crew were silent Scandinavians, but friendly enough, so that we did not feel uncomfortable. After lunch, Bob and I lazily decided to take a nap, which we did until 3:30. Then we established ourselves on the afterdeck, to enjoy the scenery, of which there was plenty! The North Shore of Lake Superior is very lonely; with only a few small villages, far apart, to break the monotony of hills and woods. Bob took a picture of me and I one of him, and I finished reading *Dot and Tot in Merryland* to him. We had supper at 6:00 and went back to our seat on the afterdeck to enjoy the almost full moon on the water. We arrived at Grand Marais at 8 P.M. and took on another passenger. After leaving this tiny town, we were glad to get to bed, for the breezes of Lake Superior were cold and strong.

September 14, 1932

We were awakened early the next morning when the boat stopped at Belle Isle, one of the most beautiful places on Isle Royale. Our first glimpse of the "Magic Isle" will always remain with us — it was a crisp, beautiful September morning, and the dark green of the woods, the clear blue of the sky, and the sparkling waters of our own lake, set off by the cream of the buildings, made a delightful picture. We received three passengers at Belle Isle, one of them a Mr. Douglas, U.S. Customs Inspector who had been stationed at Belle Isle all summer, as it is the port of entry and departure for all Canadian ships, both steamers and airships.

We went to a delicious breakfast at 6:30 hurriedly, so as not to miss seeing anything. At 7:20 we picked up reluctantly-departing summer visitors at Tobin's Harbor, and a little later, stopped at Rock Harbor Lodge to leave mail and supplies. Then we proceeded to the other end of Rock Harbor, where several hundred pounds of fish were loaded on to our boat. At 10 A.M. we landed at Chippewa Harbor, our home for the winter. It is the most beautiful place on the island, as far as I have yet seen, and we were welcomed heartily by Mr. & Mrs. Johnson and their children.

We changed clothes and simply loafed all day — had a wonderful whitefish dinner at noon. The school cabin, in which we are to live, is being made warm and comfortable for the winter, so we did not unpack in our temporary cabin. There are five children in the Johnson family, Violet, 18, Vivian 17, Gerald 12 and Holger, Jr. 10 and little Kenyon, aged 5, whom Bob immediately seized upon as the ideal companion. The children are all delightful, interesting and pleasant, and quite eager to get our school arranged and started. Conservation officer Lahti and his assistant, Mr. Larson, arrived about 7:30 P.M. with our books and baggage. Bob and I were sleepy, so we went to our cabin and to bed by 9 o'clock.

September 15, 1932 *Full moon*

We were up at 8:00. A beautiful fall day early in the morning, which changed to a squally, rainy day by afternoon. We spent the day sorting and unpacking books and writing letters to go out on Sunday's boat. In the afternoon the Rock Harbor fishermen came down, and decided to purchase a wireless for me to send occasional messages on after the boats stop running. We were all sleepy and the night turned very cold, so we got to bed early. During the night, Togo, the big collie dog, had a huge moose in front of our cabin, and in the bright moonlight, we saw a thrilling scrap between the brawn and strength of the moose, and the agility and quick-wittedness of the dog. The dog was victor, for he chased Mr. Moose ignominiously away from the tender bushes and cool water in front of our cabin back to the more common moose lunchrooms on top of the bluff back of us. We heard wolves [coyotes] calling, but serenely comfortable in the guardianship of Togo, we calmly crawled into our comfortable beds and were soon dreaming of mice and moose!

*

September 16, 1932 *N. W. wind*

This is a gorgeous day! I've set myself the task of letter writing but am going to steal time enough to climb the alluring hill back of me. I want to see all around me. The men have gone out to lift nets, so we are eager to know what luck this time.

From where I am sitting, I can look across three hundred feet of clear turquoise water sparkling in the autumn sun, at a sheer rocky cliff, peopled with the slim spires of evergreens. This is truly Isle Royale, the beautiful! I spent most of the day writing letters, but after dinner we hiked up to Lake Mason, over a very rough trail and through a real cedar swamp — hoping to see a moose, but nary a moose did we see. However, we found some lovely fungi decorations for our schoolroom as well as some sturdy small trees and felt quite exhilarated after our hike. Baths (sponge only) were in order at 4:30 and letter writing was continued.

The men lifted several hundred pounds of trout and whitefish. While we were eating dinner, up blew a beautiful Lake Superior squall — the lake was black and so was the sky and the wind whistled viciously around our cabins.

Vivian and I have decided on a rigid reducing program — dip, and hill climb and exercises twice a day, plus some dieting (impossible to do much on account of limit to variety of foods available). This big

4

program goes into effect Monday with the opening of school.

Listened to the radio until nine, enjoyed especially *The March of Time*. To bed at 9:30 — but we do our reading in bed, as it is warmer. I am reading *A New Name* by Grace Livingston Hill and like it very much, although it is somewhat improbable and unconvincing in spots.

During the night the wolves [coyotes were referred to as bush wolves] howled most vigorously on the hilltop but we had no nocturnal visitors except Jack Frost.

September 17, 1932 *N. wind, Cold, Sunny*

We were up at 8:00 and after breakfast gave our cabin a Saturday cleaning. Then I finished my letters and went over to a wonderful fish dinner — sturgeon and trout. After dinner we all wrapped up warmly and set out in the "Pep" — the eighteen foot cabin fish boat — for Hay Bay to collect the timber cruiser and his Indian guide who have been in the woods for a week, looking at timber and land for a logging company who are mercenary enough to want to desecrate our beautiful land by logging a broad strip of it. We stayed at Hay Bay long enough to eat fresh young chicken stew and enjoy a cup of black coffee, with Mrs. Anderson, wife of the fisherman who lives at Hay Bay. I found several nice agates — two large enough to cut, and Mrs. Anderson showed us her fine collection. I also learned why the point called "Fishermen's

Home" is so named. Years ago a party of fishermen were in grave danger of losing their lives in a heavy sea, when their boat was caught and tossed up at this same point; the boat was smashed into many pieces, but the fishermen walked ashore, dry and safe. The point has since been named "Fishermen's Home" by the islanders although its name on the map is Houghton Point. After leaving Hay Bay we cruised around the point to the head of Siskiwit Bay so Mr. Hartwell [stayed with the Johnsons before Dorothy Simonson] could look over the land from the boat. Then we came back to Wright's Island where we were royally entertained by Mr. & Mrs. Holte, a charming couple. The delightful custom on this island seems to be "coffee": wherever and whenever you stop — and these hospitable folks are not one whit flabbergasted by the appearance of a boatload of ten voracious passengers. Freshly baked rolls and cake and hot drip coffee made us friends of the Holtes for life! We left there at 7:30 P.M. and were home at 8:30. The "Pep" had a heavy load to carry through a big sea, but we were all good sailors and there were no casualties! The trip back was thrilling — our little boat plunging through black waves, the moon coming silently up through the clouds and the stars shining serenely above us. It seemed as if we must be in a world apart, and what a shock we received to turn on the radio and hear someone calmly speaking of WLS' *Weekly Barn Dance*! The fresh air (and a glass of good homemade beer) had made us sleepy — so Bob and I were in bed and asleep soon after 9:30.

September 18, 1932 *S. wind, Sunny*

We slept until 8:30 — didn't even hear the moose who evidently slept alongside our cabin! We saw his or her bed when we left the cabin to go over to breakfast. After breakfast we got our letters stamped and ready (I mailed thirty-three!) and at 10:00 we heard the "Winyah" blow and all hustled down to the dock to meet her. Our share of the loot was Bob's moccasins which I had forgotten Wednesday, and two letters — one from Mom and one from Martha Seaks in Chelsea. Both were much enjoyed. I'm sorry the plane manager didn't reach us, but I surely thought we had made enough "squawking" about getting over here so that everyone in the Copper Country would know about it. Mrs. Farmer left today, which means that Rock Harbor Lodge is closed for this year. After the boat left we all read letters, discussed election returns, etc., and then reluctantly turned to the prosaic task of making beds and washing breakfast dishes. Mr. Hartwell and Adam [Adam Roach, who lived with the Johnson family at Chippewa Harbor] went to Lake Richie. The flies are terrible today — simply taking huge chunks right out of our legs! We didn't do much of anything today — read and talked and listened to the radio in the evening.

September 19, 1932 *Windy, Rainy, Cold*

We worked at the schoolhouse all day. The boys

swept out and the girls and I sorted and catalogued and shelved books. We have over one hundred, in addition to our regular text books. We used the simplest form of cataloguing — just numbers and a card index. Then we fixed a corner cupboard for supplies — I started to make our "arty" new curtains — theatrical gauze, ecru, with big, splashy flowers of orange, green, and white wool — Violet made a handsome magazine rack with a roll of left-over wall paper, a packing case, and a can of green, and a can of black paint — Vivian made inkwells with vaseline and vaporizer jars and pieces of colored paper and a can of red lacquer. We planned just where all the furniture is to be placed and felt as though we had accomplished a good deal. We spent some more of Houghton Township's money in the evening — getting ready a small order for necessary supplies from the Michigan school service. Then we discussed school discipline — everyone contributing an interesting incident. Bed soon after 9:00! No moose — nor wolves [coyotes] — at least I didn't hear 'em.

September 20, 1932   *Cold, Rainy*

Worked all day in the schoolhouse. I think we will be able to get practically all settled tomorrow and can begin some work in earnest on Thursday. We plan to work right through Christmas to make up for time lost now. Mr. Hartwell leaves tomorrow and we can move our possessions up to the school as soon as he does.

Learned a Chippewa word today (from Adam Roach, our Indian guide) — ah'meek means "little beaver." Didn't do much after supper — it was cold so we all went to bed early.

September 21, 1932 *S.W. wind, Warm*

Soon after breakfast, conservation boat arrived — to wait for the "Winyah," we sat and discussed election results. The "Winyah" was late — but finally arrived about noon. Bob and I drew a package, and mail from the Lane's. After dinner we played cards as the men are working on the school today, hoping to finish it. Mr. Lahti and Mr. Larson went to Rock Harbor. Mr. Johnson is planning to go to Houghton for some of his supplies if the nice weather continues.

I wrote letters and worked on Form 9's, 10B and 2 — we are counting this week as school as we have all been working up there some.

I am anxious to hear from Mr. Winter about the "board" business: If Mrs. Johnson's understanding is correct, my salary will look much better to me.

Bob and Kenny have a "shack" up on the hill and want to sleep in it!

Started sewing on my quilt after supper — made nine "fans".

Radio reception was very poor.

September 22, 1932 *Warm, Sunny*

We washed today as the men are still working in the schoolhouse. Mrs. Johnson has a gas washing machine and a gas iron so it wasn't bad at all.

Had a big argument at lunch time about recognizing Soviet Russia — also about Mussolini. It waxed hot and furious for half an hour or so, but nothing of national moment was settled.

We went swimming about 3:00 — the water was mighty cool! However, once again we are clean!

Had the quilt fever and sewed during the evening. Went to bed early.

September 23, 1932 *N. wind, Cold*

We were up early. Bob ate only twelve pancakes for breakfast! I don't blame him — they are so good. After breakfast I gave the cabin a good cleaning up, and then attacked the ironing. We finished every bit of it and I mended and pressed all Bob's and my clothes — taking time out only long enough for lunch at 12:30, and a gin highball at 3:00!

We went trolling at 4:00, but the fish weren't having any today so came in empty-handed, but had a fine ride along the outer shore — then inside and all down Chippewa Harbor — which has many hidden surprises, and is perfectly beautiful! We saw two "sun dogs" in the sky and Mr. Johnson said that means a strong west wind within twenty-four hours.

I learned the origin of the name of another island today — Cemetery Island, in Rock Harbor, is so named because some miners are buried there, and the marker on one of the graves is still legible. Captain Bob [Ellsworth] formerly of the Conservation Department, always held a service there once a year while he was on the patrol boat, and made a wreath of wild flowers and evergreens to place on the grave.

Listened to the *March of Time* — went to bed at 9:30, all planning to arise at 6:00, and get the schoolhouse all ship-shape.

September 24, 1932

We were up at 6:30 and Bob and I hiked up to the greenstone mine before breakfast — I turned my ankle and the wolves [coyotes] howled!

After breakfast we all turned to cleaning the schoolhouse — swept, scrubbed, polished — made everything shine! Took time out for hot pea soup at noon, and went down to the fishhouse to see the day's catch. They caught a beautiful five pound brook trout in the net — are going to have it mounted.

After lunch the girls and I moved and unpacked our belongings. It took us all afternoon — with time out for beer at 3:00 — to get everything as we wanted it, but we went home to supper with the satisfaction of a "job well done."

Bob found a lovely greenstone today — we are starting our collection of Isle Royale stones very well, we think.

After supper, we sewed on our quilts and listened to music, but soon were lured to bed (after a hot bath — in a teacup!) by the sound of the sea and the rustle of trees. We are all ready to start real work Monday.

September 25, 1932

Clear and sunny, but blowing a heavy southwester on the Lake.

We were up early and waited for the "Winyah" until 12:00 — were afraid she'd had to lay over somewhere on account of the blow outside. In the meantime I began to read *Count Luckner's Story* as told by Lowell Thomas which is doubly interesting because Count and Countess von Luckner were here this summer and the Johnsons can tell some interesting little bits about them.

We saw two moose this morning — a cow and a calf, near the boys' cabin. Togo chased them before I could get a picture.

When the boat did come I had only fifteen letters and three packages. All were very interesting and entertaining. The newspaper clippings were somewhat incorrect but that is nothing unusual.

The rest of the school furniture came today and Captain Martin Christiansen of the "Winyah" very kindly donated a stove for our school. It is an unusual stove — barrel shaped. We surely do appreciate all the gifts people have been so kind as to make to our school.

After dinner we completed the arranging of our schoolroom and I made out my lesson plans for the first real work. This evening we all came home early and wrote letters. We are encountering some difficulties in establishing radio communication with the mainland but hope to get them all ironed out soon. I also wrote Bob [Dr. Robert Ashley, husband of Gretchen Ashley] to see if he could help us reach Governor Brucker in regard to the closed season October 9 — November 4, which means the difference between a comfortable winter and one of rigid economy for everyone on the island. I do feel that the people in Lansing do not appreciate the situation which these fishermen face here. Groceries come only in proportion to fish sold — and if they cannot get the fish to sell, there will not be food forthcoming — and the "Winyah" will not run after October 9 — so there we are. Well, here's hoping — and now to Count Luckner's story again!

September 26, 1932 *Cold, Rainy*

The first day of real schoolwork is over. It seemed very queer to teach so many grades with just one pupil in each grade. I'm afraid it will be hard to motivate some or much of the work under these circumstances. Also, I realize now how *little* material we really have — we are certainly operating under difficulties. The blackboard is so small and so awkward to use — the tables and chairs are all wrong for writing! Oh well — I have this consolation — it will

13

take some *real* teaching to put things across here!

I worked on schoolwork from 8:30 A.M. until 9:30 P.M. with an hour out at noon and an hour out at night. It takes studying to teach four high school subjects and four different grades in addition!

Must finish *The Sea Devil* as Mr. Lahti will be here Wednesday and it is his book.

September 27, 1932 *Warm, Sunny*

Mr. Johnson put in our stove today and we are very comfortable now. We were busy all day — there is nothing much to record as school is much the same here as it is anywhere. We did seem to accomplish something today. I ordered more seatwork supplies as I can see that they will be much needed during the winter.

Sewed on my quilt and went to bed early.

Heard over the radio that Father Klopsic died. No other news.

September 28, 1932 *Cold fall day*

School broke up in a hurry when the "Winyah" arrived this morning. We took our recess then and read mail. The letter from Mr. Winter [School Superintendent] was so curt — made me sorry I had ever written! But it was the understanding Mr. & Mrs. Johnson had which made me write. Oh well, I don't care — I always expected to have to pay my own board. But I do hope they allow us the extra equipment which is certainly much needed. We have spent so far, lamp included, if we get it, less than $40, which is certainly little enough in comparison to what these people pay in taxes.

Mailed letters to Governor Brucker and Bob today in regard to closed season.

We decided at dinner to close school this afternoon and go to Rock Harbor to discuss the radio question. Left here at 2:00 and arrived at Rock Harbor at 3:00. Visited all the folks there until 6:00. Learned the name of another island — Burnt Island — which lies off the old Rock Harbor Light and is so named because of its burned-over appearance. We took pictures of ducks on the bay, and of the islands, and of the old lighthouse. At 6:00, we again embarked on the "Pep" and went to Tourist's Home [Davidson Island] to visit Mrs. Johnson's sister. On the way, we saw a beautiful cow moose standing on the shore near the old Saginaw mine dump. I took a picture of her, but we were quite far away. After a short visit at Tourist Home, we came home over a calm lake, with stars shining serenely above. It was crisp and cold and our cozy schoolhouse seemed cozier than ever when we arrived home thanks to Mr. Christiansen's barrel stove. Baths — journal — bed. Another lovely day is over. We are still happy!

September 29, 1932 *S.W. wind, Rainy, Cold*

It was raining when we woke and how we all hated to get up. But delicious pancakes and hot coffee soon pepped us up and we started in with vim, vigor and vitality. Everyone worked hard. Our makeshift devices are pathetically amusing — Bob has to use bottle tops for arithmetic counters, and we make flash cards out of advertising cards, and stencils from candy boxes! It is a strange thing that the schoolboard does not feel able to furnish adequate equipment, when the Island folks pay some $2000 yearly in taxes.

We discussed the closed season today again. I do hope the Governor will act on the letter Mr. Johnson wrote to him. It means so very much to everyone on the island.

The men are beginning to get the winter wood. We need plenty! We worked here until 6:00 — trying to fix up some interesting seatwork for Bob and Ken, and planning next week's work for the other grades.

Had my first dish of Swedish pickled fish for supper. It is delicious — has a flavor that is mysteriously intriguing.

The girls and Bob and I had an evening of music in our own cabin. Singing with violin *obligato*! And now to bed, to read for the umpty-umth time Halliburton's *Royal Road to Romance*.

September 30, 1932

S.W. wind, Cold

Today was a very ordinary day. One would never know one was on picturesque Isle Royale — for readin', 'ritin', 'rithmetic are the same in any setting, I guess. However, we did get Jerry and Junior to sing, and had more fun. And we did have a perfectly delicious fish dinner! And we did listen to perfectly thrilling episodes in *The March of Time*. I'm sure I shall be haunted with worry over that young woman who has been kidnapped by Chinese bandits in Mankucho (?Spelling? — we don't see newspapers!) I have fourteen letters to mail and twenty-three "fans" made for my quilt, so believe I may be permitted to retire and read! Yes?

October 1, 1932

S.W. wind, Warm, Sunny

We were all up early and by 5 o'clock had finished the washing and ironing for eleven people for over a week, had washed dishes and fixed meals twice, had the house and schoolhouse spotlessly clean and Violet had baked a big batch of ice-box cookies. No accidents or casualties after the first half-hour when the "Old Faithful" gas washer almost decided to go on strike! But we coaxed him into working and all went well.

Then baths and shampoos were in order — I even had a swim (B-r-r-r - *was the water cold*!). We had the best sandwiches for supper — homemade brown bread with ham patties and lots of mustard. Dee--licious!

We enjoyed sewing and listening to the radio all evening and are going to bed with a sense of duties well done — and a pile of letters ready to be mailed when the "Winyah" blows her whistle tomorrow morning. Good-night!

October 2, 1932 — *S.W. wind, Rainy*

We were up early, and ready for the "Winyah" who brought us much mail — all our school supplies, more clothes and toys for Bobby — and letters! And I am to write for the *Detroit News* — feature stuff and pictures now — and a letter daily by radio this winter — possibly to be syndicated. I am so thrilled! Am starting right in tomorrow and will mail some script to good old Jim Ross (a true friend, indeed) on Wednesday.

Worked all afternoon at school — after I finished sputtering over Mr. Otto Sibilsky's [President, School Board] letter. That is certainly a penurious schoolboard. I'm sorry I've tried to be so economical in buying the equipment. Wrote letters all evening so as to be all set for newspaper work tomorrow. The sea is rolling in tonight — we have all been "hearing boats" today. Auditory illusions are frequent here. Just heard a wolf [coyote] howl! Chills and heart-throbs a plenty!

October 3, 1932   *S.W. wind, Cold, Rainy*

The first casualty — the schoolbell came down and gouged a piece out of Bob's nose. A nasty cut and I do hope it doesn't leave a scar. He was under the weather most of the day, so we were a little off schedule.

I worked at school until 6:00, studying and getting ready for tomorrow's work. After supper wrote script for the *Detroit News* until late.

Togo has a moose out here, but I can't see him. He is making a horrible racket, snorting!

Wonderful radio reception tonight but I was too busy to stay and listen.

October 4, 1932   *N. wind, Snow! Cold*

Our first snow which was slightly more like sleet than real snow, fell this morning. It was very cold. School went well this morning and we could scarcely realize that 12 o'clock had come. Had a wonderful fish dinner. Early in the afternoon we dismissed school to go picking wild cranberries. The small children stayed at home with Mrs. Johnson. We put on old clothes and rubber boots or galoshes, as offered by our respective wardrobes and rowed over to the point in the skiff. The whole point is a mass of flaming color set off by the dark evergreens. The sky was overcast and we could see and hear the huge rollers out on the lake which tell us fall is here.

We pulled up the boat on a little rocky shore near

the outer point and proceeded to follow the trail in to the cranberry bog. And it was a trail! We climbed over and under windfalls, over spongy moss into ankle-deep mud. I saw much beautiful moss, in great quantity, and of many varieties, also crowds of luscious oyster mushrooms, and beautiful dark red pitcher plants. After fifteen minutes of walking we reached the cranberry bog and received Mr. Johnson's warning to walk only on the hummocks. It was easy to see why — it was like walking on a giant sponge floating on deep water. Every step set the whole muskeg bed quivering. The berries are purplish in color and grow very close to the ground. Eight of us picked nearly fifty pounds in a little over an hour and the girls and I picked mushrooms, moss and pitcher plants as well. Then home again, tired, and somewhat chilly, and with decidedly wet feet. But hot coffee soon pepped us up and we enjoyed an evening writing and sewing while listening to the radio. Heard President Hoover's address — reserve my comments until after election. He did appeal to those Iowa farmers. Finished *News* stories — bed at 11:30.

October 5, 1932 *N. wind, Snow*

The boat was here at 11:30 with letters and a package of toys for Bob from Wyandotte [Ashley's home]. Lovely ones! We were busy in school until late. I was tired, so sewed and listened to the radio in the evening. It was a cold night, but beautiful with the new moon coming up over the hill, black with evergreens, and making a silver path across the water. The wolves [coyotes] howled furiously — signs of approaching winter!

October 6, 1932   *W. wind, Warmer, New moon*

We put in a day of grinding hard work in school and I continued it until a bad headache forced me to stop at 6:00. I get so discouraged. These children have been out of school so much and are weak in so many spots. However — we'll keep plugging. At 6:00, the men from Rock Harbor came in to discuss Professor Swenson's [Electrical Engineering Department, Michigan Technological University] letter. I guess we'll have our shortwave set all right. Now I must study up to get my license. Put in an evening of writing for the newspaper. It is much warmer tonight.

October 7, 1932   *Rainy, all day*

It was a good day for school work and we did work. Saw a boat way out on the horizon this morning. Mr. J. thinks it was Tormala's boat [Art Tormala ran the "Eagle," a passenger boat from Copper Harbor to Isle Royale]. He didn't stop here however. I worked at school until 6:00. Scrubbed and dusted generally.

Fixed supplies for Monday and made out some tests. After supper we listened to the radio — enjoying especially the *March of Time* and *The Little Theater Off Times Square*. It was still damp and rainy when we came home — so bed looked good!

October 8, 1932   *Rainy, Cold*

We slept until 9:30, it being Saturday and a cold rainy day. After breakfast I mended and made beds and swept — cleaned and pressed clothes. All morning we could hear a boat blowing for fog — it must have been much closer than ore boats usually come to the island.

Spent the afternoon finishing the manuscript for the *News*, and studying radio for an operator's license. In the evening we all sewed and enjoyed the radio.

October 9, 1932   *N. wind, Snow*

We were all up early and scurried around to get cleaned up before the "Winyah" arrived. She didn't come until 12:00, however! Brought us fourteen letters and five packages — two of them big Christmas boxes which we have locked away down in the lower cabin. Bob hid my birthday presents. It seemed so queer to receive Christmas packages in October.

Makes us feel truly that we are soon to be isolated.

All our mail was nice. Made me a little blue to hear about the store closing its doors, but then, we expected it. I was sorry to hear Martha Seaks' sad news. Poor girl! Life is hard!

Studied and wrote letters after dinner until 4:00, when Mr. & Mrs. John Johnson, and two young men arrived from Rock Harbor. They brought us books and magazines. We visited until 8:00, when they left. It was bitterly cold and I did not envy them their hour on the lake!

Finished my letters — and so, a'la Pepys — to bed!

(No word from the Governor. Too bad — closed season is on tomorrow!)

October 10, 1932 *N. wind, Cold, Sunny*

School went well — we worked hard until 3:00 — then the "carnival" from Rock Harbor arrived. And it's wash day too! The girls went early to entertain them. I worked at school till 6:00. They left at 7:00, and then we listened to the radio. Could hear moose snorting and wolves [coyotes] howling as we came home — the moon is nearly full, and frost-smoke is streaming across the bay. Finished my letters and mending — no manuscript this time. Glad to get to bed.

October 11, 1932 *N. wind, Snow*

A dark, dreary day. Our fire felt good. Everyone worked hard in school, and then we hurried home to help with the ironing. The wind howled around these little cabins furiously, giving a hint of what is to come. Spent the evening ironing, and listening to the radio. To bed at 10:00 — the moon is shining on a mighty chilly world!

October 12, 1932 *W. & N.W. wind, Sunny*

The "Winyah" was very late today — had to lie in a harbor during the night, as it was so stormy. Letter from Gret and more packages. Bob feels it is impossible to approach the governor now on the fish deal — too much red tape. That is true. However, I shall write it up for the *News*. We had a Columbus Day dramatization — dismissed at 3:30. The Game Wardens were here — told us how they had been treed by a moose — it also will make a good story.

Felt unaccountably blue and horrid all day. Somehow, I was discouraged — about Bob, he is acting so dreadfully— and so much to do in school and out that is just drudgery! Oh well — I ironed all evening while listening to political "hot air" and feel better, and they've brought us some wood that will burn — so that helps some. Maybe a good sleep will dispel the blues, so, as Lowell Thomas says, so long until tomorrow. (Four weeks today!) 10:30 P.M. EST.

October 13, 1932 *N. wind, Sunny*

Busy at school until 6:00 and again all evening. The men got a wolf [coyote] today, who was prowling and "howling" around our back doors early this morning. No special news to record tonight.

October 14, 1932 *Cold N. wind, Rainy*

Full moon tonight. Another busy day is over and I have just finished scrubbing and cleaning the school for one more week. I am janitor, water carrier — everything. Guess I'll try to collect janitor's wages next spring — and can I hear old Otto Sibilsky howl! Made two winter gardens and wrote two letters — one to my old friend Jon Entenza who wrote a prize story for *Liberty*. Hope he gets it — I'd like to hear from him again — we used to have fun. Listened to our favorite programs tonight — *Time* and *The Little Theater* and sewed. To bed at 10:00. An eerie night — the moon high and a roaring sea and the frost-smoke coming across the harbor. A night for ghosts to walk!

October 15, 1932 *S.E. wind, Rain*

Bob and I spent most of the day in the schoolhouse, mending, pressing, writing. Finished two stories for the *News*. We sewed all evening and I wrote one more short article for the *News*. The wind was rising as we came home and I'm thinking we're in for a storm. Heard today that Mom and Bud [Rudolph Rhines — younger brother] had left for Chicago.

We've been enjoying fresh meat this week. It tastes mighty good.

Well, one more week finished — twenty-eight to go!

October 16, 1932 *Warm, Sunny*

Well, an eventful day indeed! We were all up early and were hurrying to get the work done up before the arrival of the "Winyah" when the first major casualty of the year occurred. Kenny fell and broke his arm! He was screaming, the girls crying, Mrs. Johnson and the boys hysterical, Bob white as a sheet, and the men far away in the woods! I, for once, managed to keep my head, packed a suitcase and finished all the work, even to washing up three floors. Mrs. Johnson took Kenny to Grand Marais, leaving us to keep house. Had several letters again — the *News* wants more manuscripts and pictures — and I'll get my operator's license. Today's catastrophe showed the need for a radio.

After lunch we got into hiking clothes and the girls

and Bob and I climbed the bluff back of the house. We took pictures of the inner harbor, and of Lake Mason and its surrounding valley of pines and birches, beautiful today in the clear autumn sky. We picked much moss for our winter gardens — then came back to the house and went on to the greenstone mine on the ridge back of the schoolhouse. Bob found one lovely stone and we both found smaller ones. While we were comfortably digging away we heard loud snorting — and did we move! For the moose are in fighting trim and will attack anything they do not like the looks of. We weren't sure he'd care for us and besides, the mine is in the heart of a delectable patch of "ground pine" or hemlock [Canada Yew], a moose's favorite dessert, so we moved and how! Crashing through bushes, we scurried for the rocky lakeshore and so, back to safety. After dinner and dishes we were glad to retire to our cozy schoolhouse for an evening of reading and writing, of which this is *finis*. Good night!

October 17, 1932

Easterly winds,
Cold, Dreary, Heavy sea.

A day of work in school and out, and an evening spent writing an exam for amateur operator's license. What a job! Wish I'd had that course in Radio Communication at N.S.T.C. [Northern State Teachers College, now Northern Michigan University] this summer.

Too tired for more (1 A.M.).

Good night!

October 18, 1932 *Easterly winds, Cold*

Nothing of particular interest to record — school, study, stories to write, letters. Listened to 101 political speeches over the radio. Hot air! To bed at 10:00 — can hear the surf roar outside! Don't imagine the boat will come tomorrow.

October 19, 1932 *E. winds, Clear, Sunny*

It was such a lovely day that we hurried and washed clothes in the morning and had school too! At noon, had a message from Mrs. J. over WHDF [local radio station in Calumet] that Kenny's injury was merely a dislocation and they will be back on the "Winyah's" next trip — Sunday. We were much relieved to hear that he is OK. It gave Bob and me quite a thrill to hear the first message broadcast. Worked hard at school until 5:30 — ironed after supper. We had a terrific thunderstorm which rather spoiled the bombastic political speeches! We heard Ogden Mills (Republican) and Roosevelt, (Democrat) — and decided to vote for Norman Thomas. It is no wonder people become socialistic, or even Bolshevik in their ideas, when they have to listen to political drivel of the nature we are hearing now. And Mills mentioned all in all some 133,900,000,000 of dollars in his speech! And us with $8 or so in the bank — and $65 a month for twelve hours a day nervewracking work — to turn out more boys and girls to become more rotten, grafting, politicians. Bah!

I'm going to bed — I'd rather hear good old Lake Superior roar against the rocks than hear any more hooey.

October 20, 1932 *N. wind, Rain, Very cold*

We worked hard all day — planned a Halloween party. After supper I finished my ironing and mending while listening to the radio — we heard Norman Thomas — he wants "men, money, votes" — for the Socialist party! We heard *Omar Khayam* also — a play — liked it very much. Came home and read the *Rubaiyat.* To bed at 11:00!

Stars tonight.

October 21, 1932 *S.W. wind, Clear, Sunny*

Photographed first wolf [coyote] trapped this season.

We put in a day of hard work at school — didn't even know the game wardens had been here until we went home at noon and found the *Gazettes* [Houghton daily newspaper]. (Slightly old!)

I did my usual Friday job of scrubbing and cleaning the school. There was a perfectly magnificent sunset — black pointed evergreens against a sky shading from deepest crimson to palest pink, shot through with bars of pure gold — the lake still and peaceful, reflecting the trees and sun and the gulls cruising almost motionlessly about on its shining surface. As I watched the sun vanished in one last scarlet blaze, and wraithlike, came the frost-smoke over the lake. Darkness fell suddenly as a snuffer over a candle, and I was glad to hurry to the cabin, whose lighted windows and smoking chimney meant hot coffee and a cheery fire.

But alas for my visions of a pleasant Friday evening. Bob chose to be annoying while we were listening to Lowell Thomas and I had to paddle him. He and I came straight to the cabin, supperless, to spend a dreary evening alone. I felt exalted as I watched the sunset — now I am in the deepest depths of discouragement! Bob has always been so good — and now everything unpleasant that happens seems to be caused by him. (One feels that these people must have lived in a veritable Eden of peace, into which Bob entered as a very disturbing snake.) I have almost decided on writing to Sibilsky to send someone else here and when November 11, and end of my second month comes, depart. I can't see how I can stand a winter like this — I can't sit in this schoolhouse day and night and Bob seems to do something to bother someone every time we go down there. Not a meal do I eat in peace! And now, after a day of fatiguing mental and physical labor, I must go supperless to bed — all for $65 a month — $35 of which goes to the Johnsons for board. No wonder I feel like tying a rock around my throat and jumping in. And now I can go and haul in more wood (each piece weighs fifty pounds) to stoke this everlasting stove.

(But the fire isn't everlasting by any means.)

October 22, 1932 *N.W. wind, Warm, Sunny*

Well, I woke this morning to see the sun shining and I felt fine! All last night's gloom had vanished. We were invited to go down shore while they helped lift herring nets, and did we leave our jobs of mending and go. We went in the "Spray" — and it being one of October's choicest days, clear blue sky, shining water, breeze gently playing through the evergreens, we had a lovely ride. Past stern cliffs with their crowns of spruce and balsam, past intriguing small harbors, veritable Loreleis of interest, to lovely Huckleberry Harbor we went. Here we picked greenstones on a sun-and-lake kissed beach and collected moss for the Detroit and Chicago boxes. We found nice stones.

Then we turned north and cruised to the beach the fishermen call North Beach, about two miles north of Chippewa. Here we visited the abandoned property of the Ohio Mining Company. We found here an old iron stove, scarcely rusted at all, still holding the big teakettle in mute testimony that here once lived people like ourselves, who made tea and coffee and washed dishes, in this then-truly-isolated wilderness. There are five or six partial cabins still standing — after eighty years! One is the old blacksmith shop and on its moss covered forge we found a pair of ragged shoe soles, and the heel of a child's shoe. As we stood among the rotting logs that were once homes, I paid silent tribute to the sturdy people who had lived and loved here, so long ago, courageously facing untold hardships in a strange and almost inaccessible wilderness. We turned silently away, leaving the logs to their memories, with the tall trees a silent guard in this graveyard of human hopes and plans.

Home at 3:00 — had lunch. Then Bob and I went up in the woods for more moss and packed our boxes. Had supper (Mr. Ben Benson [fisherman], came from Malone's Island) and wrote up my *News* story — listened to the radio till 9:00 — then home and cleaned up. Feel so fine tonight — my life is easy compared to that of the women who lived here eighty years ago! Stars tonight — and warm.

(Ten years ago — my wedding day!)

October 23, 1932   *S.E. storm, Gray, Cold*

Up early and had the work all done when the "Winyah" blew at 11:00. It was rolling so that she had to back in. Kenny and Mrs. Johnson returned safe and sound and glad to be here. Received many funny letters — laughed at Sig's [Sigurd Olson, local businessman who operated a furniture store and funeral home in Calumet] Hoover jokes, plenty! — packages, etc. The books came from the Michigan State Library — a very good selection and postage only ninety-eight cents. We rearranged school this afternoon after the new shelves were put in — all set for the winter now — it looks mighty nice and cozy. Aunt Jessie's [Jessie Roche (Mrs. Andrew Roche), wife of local physician] package came also — looks interesting! Mom's letter was returned unclaimed — must have reached Chicago before she did. Mailed the boxes of moss, etc. Came up early after supper and mended and wrote and read. It is surely warm and cozy tonight, and outside the surf is roaring!

October 24, 1932 *N. wind, Rain, Cold*

A hard day — I mean we all worked hard — I stayed at school till 6:00. Listened to radio in evening. Heard Father Seifert, Ma French's friend, from St. Anne's in Calumet — he spoke about Theresa Neumann — the German mystic — the girl of the bleeding stigmata. I can't help wondering about it — Mr. Johnson laughs at it and us, but it does set one wondering. We then had a big argument about Russia. I love an argument and being fresh from school and good reading, sorta had an advantage over the rest. Anyway it was stimulating. Then home and a chapter or so of the *The Gayworthys* — to bed! Good night, everybody!

October 25, 1932 *S. W. wind, Cold, Rainy*

Nothing much to record today. Had to be hard-boiled in school — hope that will be enough for a few weeks, don't like to be cross. Sewed on the quilt again tonight. To bed early — sleepy!

October 26, 1932 *Rain, Cold*

Nothing to record — rain, rain all day — mud, slush, dirt, cold. Is Isle Royale romantic? Not today! Me for bed — a darn good place to be!

October 27, 1932 *N. wind, Cold, Snow*

Went for a walk after school but saw no moose. Took some pictures of the inner bay. We sewed in the evening — I started my map of the Middle West. Snowed quite heavily during the evening.

October 28, 1932

Furious S. E. storm,
Sleet, Cold

The worst storm in years, they tell me. It is bitterly cold, raining, hailing. The sea is roaring in, even here in the harbor. They had to move the boats over to the other side, it is pounding so here. They are worried that the fishhouse may blow away.

We listened to a play, *Mary Queen of Scots*, with June Meredith — it was good, but too short! We didn't hear *Time* because the air was cleared for Hoover's d— old speech.

It is cold here — we are all hurrying to get to bed!

October 29, 1932

S. E. wind, Snow

We woke this morning to a changed world — one covered with snow, and very beautiful. At least three inches of snow fell during the night. The children were overjoyed and spent the day making snow men and sliding on the hills. The stove was put up down in the living room, with much argument over the merits of various places for the furniture. I worked on clothes — mending and washing, did some schoolwork, wrote two stories for the *News,* and took a roll of film — went out to the point to get some of the waves, and slipped on the sloppy snow — slid and scraped my "seat"! Decided to wash my hair and thereupon did so. As I sat here drying my hair, it grew dusk and I watched the scene change from one of turbulence to one of peace and I wrote these lines:

"Against the gray breast
of the winter sky
The somber pines lay their heads
wearily.
The leafless birches
point with bony fingers
at the quiet harbor
Exhausted
In the silent dusk.
The cabins
In winter dress of white
Loom like friendly ghosts
In the twilight,
Ghosts whose friendly arms
and eyes of glowing cheer
Call me from my reverie."

Mr. Johnson came in late to supper— he had been treed for over an hour by a big bull moose, while he was out on the trap lines!

We all came up to bed early for the usual Saturday scrub up! And now it is time to say "good night."

October 30, 1932   *N. wind, Clear, Cold*

No "Winyah" as yet — she may arrive during the night!! It was storming so that we did not look for her. I did my ironing, and spent most of the day reading Willa Cather's *Shadows on the Rock* which is beautiful — fascinating — enthralling! Next summer Bob and I are going to Quebec — if the *News* pays me anything at all.

In the evening we had our Halloween party at the school — the children prepared everything — masks, food, fortunes, decorations, and invited the family. We had lots of fun — played games, told Ghost Stories, laughed until we were sick. The party seemed to be a great success — we shall have more programs and parties — gives the youngsters some responsibility and social experience as well as fun.

The girls and I cleaned up afterwards and got to bed early, as the party ended shortly after 9:00 on account of our small cherubs. Bob has a little cold — first of the season — but have doped him up well.

October 31, 1932   *N.W. wind, Rain*

What a sloppy day! The snow melted and there is mud — and more mud! I decided to order swampers for Bob — his galoshes are too small.

No "Winyah" yet — suppose he was afraid to start out in the storm Saturday.

Listened to a good democratic speech by Judge Florence Allan, and heard a mighty demonstration by New Yorkers for Hoover.

The boys visited us while we were at the house, and tied things up with seaming twine.

November 1, 1932 *N. wind, Cold, Clear*

We were awakened by the "Winyah" — I didn't even go down — received much mail and boxes galore.

Had a dreadful headache. Lahti and Larson were here on their farewell visit. Did sound funny to hear them blow "goodbye" as they left the Harbor. Made us realize that winter really is coming.

Finished up my papers for license. Mr. Swenson says I was OK with those I sent. Then I voted, but am afraid the ballots will get back too late to be counted, if the "Winyah" happens to be late next time.

Radio poor in the evening — we all have colds and sore throats, so went to bed early. I'm reading *Grand Hotel* now — impressions to be recorded later.

November 2, 1932 *N.W. wind, Cold, Sunny*

Nothing to record but work — school — cleaning, dusting, hauling wood and stoking that devilish stove! Isle Royale and its romance. Blah! It's a hunk of mud! My feet are like ice — have been writing letters all evening. There'll be no MS this winter unless that stove decides to burn — my fingers will be frozen stiff. My hands look like a coal heaver's now. Gee — I get disgusted. I worked today, in school, on schoolwork from 8 A.M. to 6 P.M. and swept the dump 'steen times — all for $65 a month! I'm too tired to write anything when night comes, after hauling and lifting one hundred pound chunks of wood for that round black devil of a stove. Oh well — six months to go! I'm looking forward to steam, hot water and a bathtub!

*

November 3, 1932 *N. wind, Clear, Sunny*

The old lake was surely rolling, all day today. I voted — hope I did it the right way! After listening to all the speeches, I was more confused than ever.

Did my ironing in the evening. The men were skinning wolves [coyotes] and minks. Oh what a smell! Today a wolf [coyote] bit Adam [Indian guide] — they had evidently not choked the creature sufficiently when removing him from the trap. Not a serious wound however.

Listened to *Omar* again — that and *Death Valley* are our two Thursday evening programs and, of course, Lowell Thomas!

*

November 4, 1932 *N.W. wind, Rainy, Half moon at night*

Nothing new to record — seven weeks of '32 over! Listened to 1001 political speeches at night. More hooey!

Finished *Grand Hotel* and liked it very much indeed. Now, I want to read it in German. Poor

Grusinskarja, wonder if she still waits in Vienna?

November 5, 1932 *N. wind, Clear, Sunny*

We slept later than usual, and then worked hard to make up for time lost. I wrote two stories for the *News*, finished a film, packed three boxes of moss for Millie [Millie Osborne — friend of family — Calumet], Aunt Jessie and Grossmama [Mrs. Frederick Smith, Houghton — Grandmother]. The woods were lovely today — I would have enjoyed staying out longer, but had too much to do — school work, mending, etc.

We had whitefish livers for dinner and were they good! Yum! All felt fine at supper and we laughed and argued and laughed some more. Now baths are in process — Bob is just getting ready for his. We expect the boat early tomorrow, so are trying to get to bed a trifle earlier.

November 6, 1932 *Fine, Warm day, Calm*

The men made a fine haul of five hundred pounds of trout and whitefish this morning! The "Winyah" brought all our winter supplies and was the dock loaded! I wonder if we'll ever eat our way out. We had nice letters and a box of delicious apples and candy from Grossmama and the girls, and a box of magazines from MacDonald's in Calumet. I was so glad to hear that Ruth [Ruth Rhines, younger sister] has a job. We are gradually deserting the "Army of the Unemployed!" Grossmama sent some papers, one of which had an article about us, so we spent most of the afternoon, discussing the "clap-trap" published about Isle Royale — one of the things I am trying to overcome in my own articles.

Spent the evening writing letters as the boat may come again Wednesday.

November 7, 1932

S. W. wind,
Stormy, Cold

We accomplished such a lot in school today. Worked on some music this afternoon too. I worked at school till after 6:00 — had supper and put Bob to bed, then wrote an article on "Wrong Impressions of Isle Royale" — and sewed. Radio was spoiled by a flood of last minute political speeches — it is perfectly sickening to have to listen to that stuff now. It is certainly raging out on the old lake tonight.

November 8, 1932

Rain,
Fierce storm outside

It was a horrible day — poured rain continuously and the whole place is a sea of mud. We listened to election returns all evening, and all are pleased that Roosevelt seems to have been chosen for our next president. And the fishermen are very pleased to hear of Comstock's (probable) election as governor.

All I care about is a decent job for next year. One that won't require wood and water hauling and janitor scrubbing and cleaning! It's fierce in this mud hole!

I'm going to crawl into bed and read old lady E. D. E. N. Southworth's *The Hidden Hand!* Just the thing for a murderous election night. We have nothing to help us make whoopee!

November 9, 1932

S.E. storm, Rain

Nothing to record but mud and rain. The place is just a sea of black slime, and the waves outside are so fierce that the whole island seems to shake.

We all came up to bed early — I intend to indulge in an evening of reading, for once!

November 10, 1932

Today was one of those discouraging days when everything was muddy, wet, smelly — the youngsters fidgety and knowing even less than usual. And after school, Bob, Kenny and the other boys got into a fight and there was much yelling and hollering — I was so darn discouraged and so sick of having a commotion all the time that I had a nice little weep all alone — when the "Winyah" blew her whistle unexpectedly and we went down to the dock to get welcome letters. Our radio set arrived! Now I am anxious to get it going — and feel much better! Spent the evening working — lesson plans, letters and a last story for the *News*.

November 11, 1932

It snowed most all day. Mr. Johnson and I set up the shortwave set and it works. I could hear Houghton, as well as many other stations. It is a fine looking, very neat and compact job and I'm beginning to get much interested in operating it. We are to have a schedule with Houghton Wednesday. Here's hoping he can read me and I him!

The children had a very nice little Armistice Day program and I dismissed them a little early. Bob stayed here and we cleaned house — then listened to the radio. After supper we sewed and enjoyed our favorite *March of Time* and *Little Theater.* Togo had a moose up on the hill — they are coming closer to our houses every day but are no longer so vicious — their antlers are beginning to fall off now.

November 12, 1932

S. W. *blow, Snow*
Full moon

Spent the day washing, ironing, mending and tapping out practice messages on the key. Read, too — took a walk out to the point. Nothing of interest to record except that Otto fell in the lake while cutting wood! Didn't bother him any though!

We have "fresh" meat — Togo won't have to bark tonight.

＊

November 13, 1932

S.W. *wind,*
Snow, Colder

We had fun sliding on cardboards on the hill today. I took several pictures. Then we came in and sewed and listened to music. Heard a good history play. Bob and I came up here at 8:00 — and the whole world looked like a gorgeous Christmas card — full moon shining on snow-covered trees and cabins, and making a path on the black water of the harbor. The inner bay is frozen over today. I took a picture by moonlight.

Have been listening in on the shortwave set — it is fascinating! And now to bed!

*

November 14, 1932   *N. wind, Colder*

The "Winyah" arrived early (10:30) — only two letters and two packages today. We received seven new books from Mr. Mathews of the Wilson Theater, Detroit — splendid books and brand new! We are grateful indeed. The "Winyah" will make two more trips.

The Rock Harbor men came down this afternoon and all are pleased with the radio set.

Listened to several good programs tonight — sewed, wrote letters and articles.

We are watching for the comet.

*

November 15, 1932   *Steadily colder*
Temp. +2

We had to "clean house" in school today after ashes blew all over everything once when the stove door blew open. Heard W9YX calling today but the key wasn't screwed in to operate. I will call him tomorrow noon. Came to bed early — did some writing. It's cold!

November 16, 1932

*Cold, Clear,
Temp. 0*

The lake was frozen over and when I went out behind the schoolhouse to empty the "pot" (about 8 A.M.), I met a huge bull moose face to face! Dropped "pot" — contents and all, and fled precipitately to the schoolhouse! But I ventured out on the porch to take a picture of the gentleman.

Tried to get W9YX at noon but couldn't raise him. I know our antenna has to be shifted — also, the "lost comet" seems to be a disturbing element atmospherically speaking.

Well I'll try for W9YX tomorrow. Came up to bed early — read and started a "boat book" for Bob for Christmas.

November 17, 1932

*S.W. storms,
Very cold*

The men changed the antenna but still we are unable to get Houghton. Today signals were fading so it was impossible to copy anyone. I listened for nearly an hour. Will try again tonight. It is so cold in here — will be glad when this storm quits. I don't like getting up at 2:00 and 5:00 to fix fires! Isle Royale is nice when the weather is — otherwise — ??? — not so!

November 18, 1932

I think I got Houghton at noon — at least I heard him call, and answered him, but it was so stormy I could scarcely hear him although he sent very slowly. I wrote to him — am wondering if I have the key adjusted correctly? Can't find any directions for it.

Listened to the radio until 10:00, then came home and got warm and read to Bob until we were sleepy.

November 19, 1932   *Still S.W., Clear, Cold*

Radio signals from everywhere except Houghton. Oh, well, I had time to get acquainted with the set anyway!

Listened to the Michigan — Minnesota game and it was a dandy, ending 3 - 0 for Michigan! Spent the evening getting ready our last batch of mail for 1932, for tomorrow the "Winyah" makes her last trip.

Temperature rising now and snow is falling softly.

Wonder whatever happened to that famous comet?!!

November 20, 1932

N.W. storm,
Heavy snow, Temp. +2

No "Winyah" today — too much snow. I sprained my shoulder carrying water and falling down so can scarcely write. We read and told stories and listened to the radio. I tried to sew — couldn't do much. Heard several good programs. C & H band from Calumet was good.

We are almost out of kerosene — hope the boat comes tomorrow!

November 21, 1932

Clear, Cold,
Temp. 0

The "Winyah" arrived at 11 A.M. on her last trip and brought us many letters and packages, but no word from the Chicago folks, nor the radio licenses. They blew five whistles and departed at 11:30 — to return April 1, or thereabouts, 1933. Bob and I watched her out of sight and took pictures of her, realizing that we are now indeed isolated. But I didn't feel nearly so "let down" as I had expected, for with a broadcast receiver and a shortwave set, we do not lack contact with the outer world entirely. And at 1:00, I had a good conversation with Operator Cook at Michigan Tech, so feel much better. Our licenses are there, so it is safe to operate now.

All our letters and packages were cheerful and interesting and will provide us with nice reading during the winter.

The *News* sent some fine enlargements of pictures. I hope I can sell an article to the *National Geographic* next spring.

Grossmama and the girls [Annie and Maria, worked for Grossmama Smith in Houghton] sent lovely boxes, as did Aunt Jessie and Sig, but we put his away for Christmas.

Enjoyed the radio tonight and now are all set for a good rest.

November 22, 1932   *Heavy S.E. storm, Temp. 0*

The world was a mass of swirling white flakes this morning and we had to break trail over to breakfast. All day the storm raged and we heard at noon of shipwrecks on the South Shore of Lake Superior.

I tried to get W9YX this noon but could not raise him. Guess this weather simply nullifies radio signals as far as we are concerned.

Bob and I went over to supper in a setting mysterious, living and yet almost threatening. For the first time we seemed to realize that we are indeed isolated on this block of snow and ice, with its threatening, fir-crowned cliffs and howling wolves [coyotes], its frozen stars and frosty moon, surrounded by nothing but a seething turbulency that men call Lake Superior. Our only link with friends and family — a little black box whose thin querulous voice sent out through frosted skies will let the rest of the world know either of our safety, or our distress. I cannot

help but wonder what the winter may bring us —
eleven people apart, with only a radio and Providence
to aid us should we need aid. I shudder as the wind
howls about this exceedingly frail shelter which we
must, for over five months, continue to call our home,
and wonder that I had the temerity to so tempt
Providence by bringing Bob, and myself, to this place,
awful and majestic, in its stand against Nature's
onslaught.

But now, I must get to bed, as we have very little
kerosene, and are not sure that we will be able to get
any at Rock Harbor if this storm ever does let up.
How that wind howls!

November 23, 1932 *S.W. storm, 8 A.M.,*
Temp. +28, Colder by night +10

We were busy all day — getting our work done in
order to enjoy our holiday tomorrow. We had a little
program in the afternoon — just stories, songs and
games. Then I decided to clean house, so did so
thoroughly. When the bell rang for supper, my work
was all done, and at peace with even my turbulent
self, I walked over crisp, crunchy snow, past trees
dark and mysterious, to cheerful conversation and
companionship. The lake was still and quiet, and in
the west only faint pink traces remained where
shortly before had been a brilliant kaleidoscope of
color. Gulls were motionless on the black water and
far off in the hills, a wolf [coyote] called to its mate. I
gave thanks for beauty of the world about me, and

stood a moment, silent, thoughtful in the presence of the majesty of Nature.

Radio tonight sort of bothered me — much talk of home and much singing of *"Home, Sweet Home,"* which always was my musical waterloo! And so to *Innocents Abroad* and a warm bed!

✳

November 24, 1932   *Strong S.W. winds, Temp. +32*

Well, our Thanksgiving Day on Isle Royale is over! And it wasn't half-bad! I washed my hair and sat in the big rocking chair and read *The Door* while my hair dried, in the morning. We had dinner at 2:30 — whitefish, sweet potatoes, cranberry sauce, beets, onions in vinegar, fresh rolls, pumpkin pie and coffee. (Oh, yes — and "Isle Royale turkey" [moose] for those who don't like fish as well as I do!)

We went sliding on the hill in the afternoon and had heaps of fun. Then we came in and sewed and gabbed and listened to football games and so passed the day, with coffee and fruit cake (from Houghton) — and now to bed!

This Thanksgiving was happier than last year's because my mind is at peace this year. And so, although we missed all the folks, still we can truthfully say "Let us give thanks!"

November 25, 1932

S.W. winds,
Temp. +10

We worked hard until 11:00 — then started out in the "Pep" for Rock Harbor in search of kerosene. It was rolling plenty outside, but Bob and I liked it and were so disappointed when Mr. Johnson decided it was rolling too much and turned back. I did take some good pictures though.

After lunch we sailed in and did a heap of school work. And so to the evening — and our favorite programs. Togo had a moose outside last night — but it was so dark all I could see was a huge shape!

November 26, 1932

S.W. winds,
Temp. -2

Winter is here! The temperature has fallen below zero and the bay is frozen solid.

Bob and I were thrilled to get messages over WHDF at noon — one from Professor Swenson, answering my questions about the key, and one from "all my friends" in the Copper Country.

We worked all day — doing the washing, some ironing, and mending. I am so tired now and it is darn cold since our fire went out! And so, a bath (in a teacup) and to bed!

Twenty-two weeks to go!

November 27, 1932

Still S.W. winds,
Much warmer, Temp. +32

Nothing much to record as we spent a peaceful Sunday reading, sewing, writing, with an hour of coasting on the hill. We nursed our old black "F.F." all day, so it is nice and warm tonight and I am enjoying Mazo de la Roche's *Jalna.*

I forgot to mention last night that we heard WWJ's Sunday reporter tell about my story of the wolf [coyote] biting Adam. And were we thrilled to hear it! Fame (not Fortune, however) is ours!

November 28, 1932

N.W. winds,
Rising temp. +40

Nothing to record but a day of schoolwork and planning for Christmas which lasted from 9 A.M. until 11 P.M. with an hour out for eats. And all for $65 a month! I know I'm crazy, but there are so many things I'd like to accomplish in this term. I'm hoping to pull Jerry and Junior through two grades, and Bob likewise. So, with four high school subjects, and a slow first-grader and all the janitor work I have to move! Haven't had time to listen in on the short-wave set in days. Oh, well — time flies!

November 29, 1932

S.W. winds,
Temp. +50

My thirtieth birthday is over! I enjoyed it very much, as it was a lovely warm day without, and everything went exceptionally well within. Bob and I opened my gifts and cards in the morning, which made me a trifle blue and lonesome.

Violet made a lovely chocolate cake, with Happy Birthday in code, and the family here gave me a perfectly beautiful greenstone. We had a lovely supper and spent the evening listening to the radio.

It was a very nice birthday — and now, I guess I can't have any more!

November 30, 1932

S. wind,
Temp. +60

The snow has nearly all melted and the air is positively balmy. It was hard to stay in school on such a nice day.

Received another message from Swenson over WHDF and tried to get Houghton between 1:30 and 2:00 — heard everyone else, but no Houghton! I will try again tomorrow. That set is making me horribly nervous. I hope I can get a good contact with Houghton tomorrow.

December 1, 1932

It was such a lovely day that the folks decided to pay their final visit of the year to Rock Harbor. As it is necessary, on Isle Royale, to take advantage of the weather, we agreed to take the day off, and all go.

After we started, we found a much heavier sea than appeared from here, but we kept on rolling and swaying from side to side. Just before we reached Saginaw Point, the skiff broke loose and we had to lie in the trough of the sea, after making a sharp turn almost on the side of the boat. But everyone sat still and said nothing, so we managed to get righted and proceed. By this time, the sky had turned gray and lowering, and I, for one, felt like a mighty insignificant atom in the scheme of things, pitching and tossing in a twenty foot cockleshell on Lake Superior, whose giant fist seemed to pick us up and shake us as a baby shakes its rattle!

We reached Rock Harbor about 11 A.M. and went over to the old Light House where we visited until 3 o'clock. Vivian and I climbed up in the old tower — the view from there is gorgeous.

The men decided they'd like to go on to Rock Harbor Lodge and visit the caretaker and his family there, so we loaded everyone on to the boat and started out. I took a picture of the Indian Head [a rock formation near Edisen Fishery]. We picked up three more passengers at Tourist Home [a small resort on Davidson Island] and went on to the Lodge. It was beautiful traveling through the December dusk over a calm harbor, with the snow-coated trees looking ghostly and vague, as darkness swiftly fell. We finally arrived at the Lodge and there they decided to go over to the dining room and have a dance. Violet and I furnished the music on a worn-out violin and an awful old piano. We played Scandinavian schottisches galore! It was a great dance — the men all wore their hats, lumber-jackets and rubber boots! The little kids all bawled when their mothers danced!

We started home at 11:00, and when we ran in to Tourist Home to deposit the John Johnsons [John (Holger's cousin) and Lorraine (Lucy Johnson's sister) Johnson], Otto Olson [Holger's cousin and fishing partner who lived with the Johnson family at Chippewa Harbor] misunderstood the signals and ran the boat on shore. We all had to move to the back of the boat, and then Mr. Johnson tried to get the boat off the rocks. Otto tried to handle the rope, and he and Mr. Johnson had a fight while we all huddled in the back of the boat. I was scared, and so was Bob. But Mr. Johnson finally squelched Otto and got the boat going. We dropped the rest of the crowd at the Light House and turned on and out into the lake. It was still rolling, but not so noisily or what-have-you as in the morning. We had a pleasant trip home and arrived here, singing *There's No Place Like Home*, at 1 A.M. I put Bob to bed — he was so tired — the rest of us had lunch and went on to bed. I was so glad to be there!

December 2, 1932

S.W. wind,
Temp. +60

Had a schedule with W9YX at 1:30 — their signals swang so it was impossible to copy, but we arranged a schedule for Monday. Put up some Christmas pictures and planned some Christmas work. Listened to 100th anniversary play of the *Little Theatre*. It was good!

December 3, 1932

S.E. gale!
Temp. +10, Snow

Worked all day on Christmas gifts. It turned much colder and snowed a good deal. We worked until 1 A.M.!

December 4, 1932

S.E. wind,
Temp. +10, Snow

What a day! I experimented nearly all day with the shortwave set. Mr. Johnson helped me. It is OK on the receiving end but no good on transmission. I was so discouraged I simply went to pieces — but I've done all I know to make it work and that's that. Well, I'll try Houghton again tomorrow and hope for the best.

Now to do some more Christmas work and get to bed early!

✳

December 5, 1932

*S.E.wind,
Temp. +10, Sunny*

Well, I heard Houghton — started to answer him and the whole blamed key fell apart! However, that is repaired and here's hoping for better luck tomorrow.

We did work today — much Christmas work was accomplished.

Congress vetoed beer! Well!! And we argued Russia again tonight — as usual settling nothing.

S.W. tomorrow — radio poor!!

✳

December 6, 1932

*Winter and How!
Colder, Temp. +5*

WHDF broadcast Mrs. Champney's article today, for us — she used all my stuff to suit herself, and distorted some! However, it was fair. But I'd rather she'd have printed it as was.

WHDF's staff sent us all best wishes. I tried to get Houghton to thank them, could hear him perfectly but he said our signals were so faint he couldn't read them. Well, all radio is no good here today — so will

58

try again tomorrow.

*

December 7, 1932

*Strong N. winds,
Temp. -8*

Is it cold! The school is positively barnlike. I've worn two pair of wool hose and still my feet are like chunks of ice! We have had a good fire but there is no foundation under the floor. Enough said!

Received another message from Professor Swenson — we have already removed the switch but Mr. Johnson went over the key and found a loose terminal and a loose plug. Will try again tomorrow.

*

December 8, 1932

*S.W. gale, Blizzard,
Temp. -20*

What a day! Stormy — cold — the school is like a barn and all of us huddled around the stove which simply gobbled wood.

I tried Houghton again — heard half a message or so — then he faded completely. Guess there is still something wrong with our transmission. Well, I'll wait till Saturday now — have too much to do in school to monkey with that during the day.

I did my Christmas sewing in bed with my feet on a hot water bottle!

December 9, 1932

*N.W. wind, Sunny,
Temp. -8*

Isle Royale was beautiful today — trees bedecked in white, and a crisp crunchiness to the snow.

It was plenty cold — inside as well as out. We changed the furniture about so more people can be close to the stove.

The third month of school ended today — five to go!

No radio tonight — all batteries were either dead or frozen!

December 10, 1932

*S.W. wind,
Much warmer, Temp. +12*

We did a land-office job in the clothes-washing line, as it was much warmer.

Had a nice letter from Mom and the kids which was read over WHDF at noon. They are all going to Wyandotte for Christmas — and will we envy them! I'm glad they'll all be together anyway.

Tried to get W9YX at intervals during the afternoon, but no luck.

We have practically finished the doll's house which we are making for our dear little "girls" for Christmas.

"Tim and Tena" were good tonight — (I'll never forget "when Caesar burned his pants!")

To bed by moonlight — shining over a frozen bay and trees dressed in glistening white.

60

December 11, 1932

S. wind, Warmer, Temp +20, Snow

We had a lovely peaceful Sunday — snow fell gently all day long and Bob and I spent the day doing Christmas work in the school. I feel that we are truly possessed of the Christmas spirit, for we are having a grand time making many gifts of little cost. Violet, Vivian and I are making a three room house and furniture of pasteboard cartons — Violet made the furniture — I made curtains, a real patchwork quilt, etc. Today Bob and I made book marks, pen-wipers, address books — everyone has a secret and is working very busily at something and it's fun! The boys are doing a beautiful winter garden for their mother — and some hand-tooled leather things (out of an old purse of mine) — for the men.

Heard another splendid history play — the scrap between the "Monitor" and "Merrimac".

A heavy sea rolling again!

December 12, 1932

S.W. wind, Temp. +5

Houghton (W9YX) keeps telling me not to use the side switch on key — and we have removed it (ages ago) so we are at a loss to know what to do. Oh, well!

A good day — much accomplished. And good radio at night. We laughed until we were sick over *Nana, Cyril and Patty!*

To bed by brilliant moonlight.

December 13, 1932

S.W. wind,
Temp. -2

Nothing to record today — worked, made Christmas gifts, read. I finished making Kenyon's "Book of Cars" tonight. He will little suspect that my Christmas gift is designed to "motivate" letter-learning! (Oh, shades of Ruthie Teeters!)

December 14, 1932

N.W. wind, Blizzard,
Temp. -10

A howling blizzard and falling mercury reminded us that winter is here. And we used much wood.

Again W9YX tells me to remove the switch, which I did two weeks ago. We removed another little gadget — here's hoping!

Worked all evening making Bob's boat book which is truly a fascinating job. I'm giving every boat a name. More fun!

December 15, 1932

N.W. wind,
Temp. -14

Well, we had messages over WHDF today. And, praise be, W9YX OK'd today! Don't know what we did, but he can read me now. I am so darn glad — not for myself so much — because I don't expect anything to happen to tough Bob and me, but because there is $60 tied up in the set and it seems too bad not to get results. (France defaulted today!)

December 16, 1932

S.W. winds,
Temp. -12 to +18 to -14

No battery today. So no W9YX — well, that's tough luck! Mr. Johnson did manage to charge batteries for a little while although he had plenty of trouble thawing out the engine.

The harbor is frozen way out past the store now.

The thirteenth week of school is over! (Thank Goodness!) Nineteen to go.

Good radio tonight.

December 17, 1932

S.W. wind,
Temp. +2

The ice was all gone from the harbor today.

Didn't get our batteries charged in time to get W9YX today. It is so hard to charge them as the engine freezes constantly.

I made the winter garden we are giving Mrs. Johnson — painted various plants, etc., to give it color. It is really pretty. And one of the narcissus bulbs is about ready to blossom.

We wrapped gifts in the evening. Our packages look nice — paper is cheap — even if the gifts are makeshifts.

December 18, 1932

S. wind,
Temp. +18

A perfectly gorgeous day! We took pictures, but I had so much Christmas work on hand that I didn't get out much.

We enjoyed so much the American Legion broadcast from Calumet. It was mighty nice of Mike Smith to remember us over here. It seemed like going home to listen to that program — Paul Peterman singing, etc.

We didn't enjoy the history play so much this week — guess it was too tame!

December 19, 1932

S.W. wind,
Temp. +22

A beautiful day! The world was so quiet and beautiful this morning that Bob and I stopped on our way to the house and enjoyed just living.

The "Dagmar" and Rock Harbor people arrived at noon. We tried to get Houghton with a bunch of messages but failed. The set seems to be working OK — I spent most of the afternoon working on it. No use!

Evening in Paris and *Dr. Fu Manchu* were good tonight.

Bob and I had a letter from Mom and the kids today via WHDF. They have moved to 311 N. Central Avenue.

I made two cedar wreaths, with red bows and lacquered pine cones — tonight.

December 20, 1932

S.W. wind,
Temp. +32

No news — battery died out as I was trying to get W9YX.

Made my creche after school — it is pretty even if it is made from makeshifts.

Spent the evening writing lesson plans — doing Christmas work.

We have some moose hanging around here now — they like the taste of our woodpile.

December 21, 1932

No news — no battery! Bob and I cleaned and decorated the school and trimmed the tree. School looks nice.

Went to bed early — quite all in!

*

December 22, 1932

I managed to get W9YX long enough to send messages to George Burgan, Grossmama, and the family at Wyandotte. Will have to finish the telegrams tomorrow as my ears played out today.

There were moose tracks all around our woodpile this morning.

*

December 23, 1932

A gorgeous day — warm and sunny. We heard WHDF say they would send messages to us at 1:15 Christmas Day. I tried in vain to reach W9YX today — no luck at all — the battery played out!

Made and filled little red boxes with different kinds of candy tonight.

December 24, 1932

S.W. wind,
Temp. +40

We were busy all day with final Christmas preparations. The men started out in the boat to get Ben Benson [Malone Island] but had to turn back — it was too rough.

I tried all day to get W9YX, and finally picked him up, but there is something so loose in that set that it is impossible to hear him. I sent the telegrams but the battery died before I could get an OK.

We sat up and listened to the radio until late — tried to get Calumet but another station drowned them out.

December 25, 1932

N.W. wind, Snow
Temp. +10

Christmas on Isle Royale! We were awake at 8:00 when the men started out to get Ben. I wonder how many boats were on Lake Superior today? It was rough, but they didn't want Ben to spend Christmas alone, so went the eight miles down and eight back to let him in on a little of our Christmas fun.

And we did have fun. We all had gifts, lovely ones — even our school-and-homemade creations making a brave showing! Bob's and my gifts from home were grand! So were the ones we had from the folks here.

The men returned about noon and we had lunch. At 1:45 we heard our messages from WHDF — were so tickled. Bob and I had messages from Mom and kids, the Ashleys, the Knapps, the Raleys, and Sig and Lila, — also heard that we are to have a weekly news broadcast every Saturday 1:15 E.S.T., especially arranged by *Time* and WHDF! We were disappointed because no mention was made of our greetings. Evidently W9YX didn't deliver the messages he OK'd for — I feel just sick about it. However will try some night this week to send to someone else.

We had dinner at 5:00 and spent the evening playing cards (Hearts) and had lunch at 1:30.

I read part of *The Crystal Pagoda* last night — it is good!

December 26, 1932

S.W. gale,
Temp. +10

A lazy day until late afternoon when the men removed ashes from the schoolhouse stove and then I spent the rest of the day scrubbing and cleaning the rooms which I had cleaned thoroughly twice last week. Was I disgusted!

December 27, 1932

S.W. wind,
Temp. +23

Back to school again — and glad of it!
A belated Christmas message today — from

Grossmom and the girls which had been mislaid in WHDF's office! I thought it was strange not to have heard from them.

*

December 28, 1932
N. wind, Temp. +3

No news — nothing to record — the men took Ben back to Malone Island and I started writing exam questions.

*

December 29, 1932
S.W. wind, Temp. +23
121 days left to stay here

Bob and Kenny proceeded to disobey all orders and Bob fell in the lake — came home dripping wet and was promptly sentenced to bed. Supper here for him! It is much too cold to try swimming in Lake Superior now.

I am reading Theodore Dreiser's *The Genius* now — it is very fascinating, especially from a psychological viewpoint.

How the wolves [coyotes] did howl early this morning. My blood ran cold, for they seemed to be so near. They were evidently devouring a moose, for their howling was fiendish!

December 30, 1932

N. wind, Snow,
Temp. +3, 120 days

End of the fifteenth week of school. No news today. Everything quiet except the wind which is "Y-o-oo-ing" plenty!

December 31, 1932

S.W. gale,
Temp. +28, 119 days

No news — terrific wind storm and much school work preparatory to exams and closing the semester. We were disappointed in not having our news broadcast from WHDF — guess something must have prevented it. The New Year came in unwatched by anyone here, as batteries died and we had no radio to keep us up. I hope the wind which blew the New Year in will blow some of our troubles away.

January 1, 1933

S.W. storm,
Temp. +23, 118 days

Seventeen weeks from today, Bob and I will depart — we hope.

Our stove celebrated the New Year by acting "ornery"! Bob and I made puzzles, played ten pins, ring toss and read during the early part of the day.

Bob is beginning to learn to read music and can play a tune or two on his mouth organ, also on his lovely accordion!

*

January 2, 1933

S.W. wind,
Temp. +30, 117 days

No news except that the generator for charging batteries is broken, so there will be very little radio unless they can borrow one from Rock Harbor, weather ever permitting a trip there. This is a real tragedy, for it means no more news, entertainment or communication! When one is so dependent on radio as we have to be, it is truly tough luck!

*

January 3, 1933

S. wind,
Temp. +60, 116 days

A beautiful day — almost springlike. We rearranged school furniture — still trying to make for the utmost efficiency with our makeshift equipment.

Tomorrow semester exams begin — then we begin the homeward stretch. (Thank Goodness.)

There was a gorgeous sunset tonight.

January 4, 1933

The first day of our three of exams is over. Results so far are very satisfactory, as the marks were all good and we have completed five months' work in less than four months!

Bob is all set for Grade Three, second semester!

*

January 5, 1933

Another day of exams over! We learned with sorrow of the sudden death of Calvin Coolidge, who was indeed a good president.

My map is almost finished [Embroidered map of the Midwest, with designs depicting farming, industries, state flowers, etc., for each state]!

*

January 6, 1933

Sixteen weeks of school are completed! On the whole I am quite satisfied with results.

The girls and Otto walked to Rock Harbor today, to spend the weekend.

January 7, 1933

N. wind,
Temp. 0, 113 days

Nice message from Mom today. It made us lonesome for all of the family, but especially Joanne and Janet [Daughters of Dr. & Gretchen Ashley, Wyandotte, Michigan]. We learned that Grossmama had received our message at Christmas, but cannot understand what happened to the rest of the messages! I hope I can get a contact with Dr. Knapp's friend, but until our generator is fixed, I have no battery.

The second mystery is, what happened to the *News* program we were to have? Nary a sound have we heard about it since the announcement on Christmas day. Many unsolved puzzles!

Today was a crisp, fine day, but having no snowshoes, and much work, I had to be out very little. But we have planned to get out tomorrow and walk some.

January 8, 1933

N. wind,
Temp. +6, 112 days

A nice day — walk, pictures and lots of sewing done. The girls, Otto and Jack B. [Jack Bangsund, fisherman from near Edisen Fishery whose cabin was later used as headquarters for the moose-wolf ecology research program] came about 2:30. We spent the rest of the day sewing and talking and listening to the radio. I worked jig-saw puzzles after Bob went to bed.

January 9, 1933

*N.E. wind,
Temp. +3, 111 days*

After a day of good hard work in school, we were settled by a cozy fire, with our sewing, and listening to some of our special favorite programs on the radio, when suddenly (about 9 P.M.) we heard a boat and rushed to the windows to see it docking. When one feels completely isolated, it gives one a shock indeed to have a boat arrive at night.

The boat proved to be the "Dagmar" from Rock Harbor, and they had come for help as Mrs. Lorraine Johnson (Lucy's sister) at Johnson Island was very ill. I packed all our medicines and at 9:30 Mrs. J. and I set out on the "Dagmar." It was cold, and rolling plenty — but a brilliant, moonlit night. The "Dagmar" is a sixty-three foot boat but she seemed to hit bottom more than once on one of the old Lake's big rollers.

We arrived at Johnson Island [Star Island] about 11 P.M. and found Mrs. Johnson really very ill with acute gastritis. She had almost no temperature but a very weak pulse and a gray look about her face. We placed hot water bottles around her and gave her Citrocarbonate and later, calomel. By 12:30, she was feeling better, and so we took turns sleeping on a hard davenport.

January 10, 1933

S. wind,
Temp. +42, 110 days

Spent the day alternately reading and dosing the invalid who began to show signs of recovery. By night she was quite comfortable.

*

January 11, 1933

N. wind,
Temp. +5, 109 days

Mrs. Johnson was much better. We gave her gruel and broth and she gained considerable strength. We hoped to start home in the afternoon but no one came for us.

*

January 12, 1933

No wind,
Temp. -10, 108 days

When we woke in the morning we were horrified to find all Rock Harbor channel frozen solid! All morning Mr. Johnson and his son tried to break ice so we could get out into the open lake with the rowboat and row the two miles to Rock Harbor [Lodge]. But no chance! It was impossible to break through. We were beginning to wonder how in the world we were ever to get home! But at 3:15, our own Chippewa Harbor men, with the little "Pep" were seen trying to break through into the channel. They tried three places and finally managed to get into Davidson Island, which lies about a quarter of a mile from Johnson Island. They came over in the skiff breaking ice with an ax, we had hot coffee and rowed over to Davidson Island, walked through snow up to our knees, fell through ice, and finally boarded the "Pep". Even the outer lake had its coating of ice by now, and it was a sight I shall never forget to see the little "Pep" valiantly breaking through to take us home! The moon rose and the ghastly frost-smoke surrounded us, as the temperature steadily fell. Home and hot coffee awaited us — and perhaps the biggest thrill of the whole journey was the light in the window as we broke through the three inches of ice in Chippewa Harbor. The "country doctors and their hospital" were at home! And best of all, their patient was well on the road to complete recovery and the dreaded trip to town in zero degree weather was once more staved off! So endeth another adventure.

January 13, 1933 (Fri. too!)

N. wind,
Temp. -32!, 107 days

A cold night and day. Wow! We sat around the stove in school huddled together as closely as possible, trying to keep warm.

Decided that all hands would turn to and clean house (school) in the afternoon to get warm.

And — at night — sad but true — I had one sweet attack of pleurisy. Oh, me!

January 14, 1933

S.W. gale,
Temp. +20, 106 days

We had our first *Times* broadcast from WHDF today and enjoyed it very much. Bob and I also had a letter from Mom — learned that Bud has a job! Hope he likes it and sticks to it.

We finished another jig-saw puzzle this afternoon. Have done all of them now so I can get at my sewing in peace. Those puzzles are too fascinating to let alone.

Pleurisy still on the job — I'm about to have a hot mustard foot bath and try to vanquish it.

How that wind does roar — and wolves [coyotes] are howling very near tonight — fresh meat! It makes my blood run cold!

January 15, 1933

N. wind,
Temp. +20, 105 days

Mama's birthday and I couldn't send her a message — we have no batteries! The generator only charges enough so we can get news and an occasional program.

Have only a day's work left to do on my map.

My friend "Pleurisy" is reluctantly leaving me, I believe.

January 16, 1933

N. wind,
Temp. +10, 104 days

Nothing to record — all quiet on Isle Royale except the wind and wolves [coyotes]!
Evening in Paris was hair-raising!

January 17, 1933

N. wind,
Temp. 0, 103 days

We had the rest of the *Time* program from WHDF today and enjoyed it very much.

January 18, 1933

S.W. gale,
Temp. +18, 102 days

A beautiful spring-like morning turned into a raging, roaring gale, with sleet and hail by afternoon. We had to sit up and watch our fire as we were afraid to stoke up too much with such a wind, and yet could not let the fire go out entirely.

January 19, 1933
N.W. wind,
Temp. +28, 101 days

Tonight I finished my "Map of the Middle West"! If only the next hundred days would pass quickly. We're tired of Isle Royale. Wind, sleet, snow, school — no radio! Oh, well!

January 20, 1933
S.W. wind,
Temp. +18, 100 days

Another school week over — fourteen to go. I am really awfully tired — too much work and not enough play. I planned my quilt design and will start sewing the fans on to the blocks tonight.

January 21, 1933
S. wind,
Temp. +38, 99 days

Mr. and Mrs. Johnson and Jack [Bangsund] walked to Rock Harbor today. I had Jerry and Junior in school catching up on some back work. Started some more spring sewing.

Heard our *News* program from WHDF today — enjoyed it a lot. We do appreciate Mr. George Burgan's kindness!

No radio at night — the battery died in the middle

of *Tim and Tena.*

Started Lila's cookbook and wrote the story of our trip to Johnson Island.

January 22, 1933

S. wind,
Temp. +40, 98 days

A lovely day — but too soft for walking so the girls and I sewed all day long. Hope my eyes don't go too haywire from so much reading and sewing!

January 23, 1933

S.E. wind,
Temp. +20, 97 days

The Rock Harbor crowd arrived on the "Dagmar" at noon, we had school until 3 P.M. anyway!

We have a new generator and battery. The Rock Harbor people stayed until 6:30 — then we had a nice peaceful evening sewing, and with good radio. I have eleven blocks out of forty-eight made for my quilt.

January 24, 1933

S.W. wind,
Temp. +20, 96 days

A nice fall on an icy trail made me hobble about with a semi-sprained knee and back. First casualty for some time!

January 25, 1933

N.W. wind,
Temp. +30, 95 days

A beautiful day! The lake blue and calm — we were tempted to go somewhere in the boat but resisted the temptation and worked hard instead.

A cow and a calf moose crossed the ice of the bay this morning (fascinating). We all rushed out to see them.

Tim & Tena were good at night. One of Bob's front teeth is about ready to drop out.

January 26, 1933

N. E. wind,
Temp. +10, 94 days

A hectic day! Bob slow in school today — the rest fighting with each other and lazy. And I, with a bad headache, as usual, on account of the wretched lights by which we have to work, and it is snowing, cold, windy — all in all, a day I'll be glad to say farewell to!

January 27, 1933

No news. Otto and Adam came home from Malone Island and Siskiwit Bay. The folks that way are all well.

Thirteen weeks more of school! We have loads and loads of snow.

✳

January 28, 1933

S.W. wind,
Temp. +10, 92 days

A busy day sewing, washing, ironing. Had our program at noon — heard interesting details about some items of real interest and importance.

Mr. Johnson started a model log-house 20" x 20". Otto is working on Bob's big sailboat. The rest of us are making quilts and spring underwear.

✳

January 29, 1933

N.E. wind,
Temp. +22, 91 days

Well, today is a black and sorrowful day for all of us for at one o'clock we heard that WHDF is to be closed Tuesday night, for three months, probably permanently. It was like hearing of a death in the family. Perhaps none of WHDF's listeners will feel its loss so keenly as we on Isle Royale! WHDF to us was a friend, interested and sympathetic. Now indeed are we cut off from friends and home until the boat comes, for we have no battery strong enough to use on our own W9BL. We were all gloomy and sad today — it is with real and sincere sorrow that we mourn the passing of a friend, WHDF!

We are hoping the "Winyah" will come in March now. Are having to begin to count and mete out supplies, at home and in school, in order to make them last.

January 30, 1933

N.E. wind, Snow,
Temp. +22, 90 days

Nothing of interest to record except that Jerry finished his large map of the U.S. and it now hangs proudly on the east wall of the schoolroom.

January 31, 1933

S. wind,
Temp. +40, 89 days

Received messages at noon for the last time — one from Mom — she will try to communicate with us through CKPR at Fort William — says Joanne had pneumonia but is better. Also a message from Mr. Swenson, giving us our new call, W9LFP and arranging a new schedule, also suggesting that we look over the antenna for breaks. Then George B. gave us his personal "good-bye" and we all cried — it seemed like saying a long good-bye to a friend!

Mr. J. and I tested the shortwave set — found everything OK apparently — I tuned in and heard W9YX calling me, answered him, and lost him — he just faded out of the picture. I sent a message to him for WHDF, hoping he'd get it but don't know. There is certainly a leak somewhere in that set — but where we don't know. We are anxious to write to Mr. Swenson now and check up on it. It may be the location, also.

We listened to WHDF's "sign-off" at 8:30 — they introduced all the staff members, including "Uncle Ole." We all wish the station good luck and hope for its speedy return to the air!

February 1, 1933

*S.W. wind,
Temp. +20, 88 days*

Had a fairly satisfactory contact with W9YX today but his signals fade and blur so that it makes him very difficult to read.

February 2, 1933

S.W. *wind,*
Temp. +5, 87 days

The Ground Hog saw his shadow, so we get six weeks more winter.

A monotonous day — nothing to record!

＊

February 3, 1933

S.W. wind,
Temp. -2, 86 days

Nothing new today — report cards for the fifth month — only three more to go.

No battery — so no radio of any kind.

＊

February 4, 1933

N. wind,
Temp. -4, 85 days

Adam, Otto and John Skadberg [fisherman, Hay Bay] walked from Hay Bay (twenty-five miles today) — all are well there but have none too much food.

We sat up late listening to the barn dance. I've about finished the yellow nightgown.

85

February 5, 1933

N. wind,
Temp. -18, 84 days

Cleaned ashes from our stove today — I carried out forty-two shovelsful, which meant the rest of the day was spent cleaning house. I finished the yellow nightie after supper, also made some Valentines.

We thought we heard the "Winyah" today — almost had heart failure — but guess it was only the wind, as we all rushed out to the point, but saw nothing! We are often hearing boats and airplanes. It must be that the silence affects us strangely. Last night I lay awake listening to the ice cracking in the bay, and the owls torturing a rabbit up in the woods until I could hear almost anything.

We have only twelve weeks of school left — have to make knots [nautical term for miles covered within one hour] now — but I think we will finish a ten month course in seven and one-half months, which is not a bad record after all.

*

February 6, 1933

N. wind,
Temp. -32!, 83 days

Was it cold today! The harbor is frozen way out now and the place looks like an Arctic waste — ice and snow everywhere!

We burned plenty of wood today but managed to keep fairly warm except our feet, as floors here are <u>cold</u>.

Had much jollity in the evening — many jokes and wisecracks. The cold outside seemed to warm up everyone inside, and did we all enjoy a good laugh!

*

February 7, 1933

*N. wind,
Temp. -40! 82 days*

The coldest day so far. Even "Hay" was frozen solid this morning! And we had a good fire all night — I was up every two hours. We had to hug stoves today — managed to keep tolerably warm except for feet. These cabins are not built for cold weather like this! Decidedly are not "air" tight.

The bay is frozen clear out to the points now and when we go down to get water, it seems like going out on an Arctic ice waste — snow and ice everywhere.

It is too cold to charge batteries so we are without radio. Well, I guess I'll get the "wot hater bottle" as Bob says, stoke up old F.F. and get <u>dressed</u> to go to bed. (Have to wear more then than during the day!)

*

February 8, 1933

*N. wind,
Temp. -29, 81 days*

Still bitterly cold. We hugged the stoves and drank coffee to keep warm — managed to have school, though and no casualties except darn cold feet!

The temperature dropped to -42 during the night.

✻

February 9, 1933
N. wind,
Temp. -38, 80 days

This was the coldest day yet — 38 below at noon (all my recorded temperatures are noon-day or high point temperatures). We suffered plenty with cold feet today. Hope this cold spell soon leaves us.

The bay and lake, way out, are frozen solid. We have to chop holes to get water.

✻

February 10, 1933
N. wind, Full moon
Temp. -43, 79 days

Well, this was the coldest yet — a blizzard besides. We had to hang blankets and carpets across the door and windows in school to keep warm as well as move all furniture as close to the stove as possible. We burned thirty huge birch logs during the day and still were cold! We finished up early, by 2 P.M. — as the house is warmer than it is here. Bob, Vivian, and I cleaned the school and were mighty glad to fill up on hot coffee when we finished. Bob wore six pair of hose and I three! Mrs. Johnson says this is the worst winter (as to weather, I mean) of any she has yet spent on the island.

The wind shifted to southwest in the afternoon, but that made the schoolhouse colder than ever, as we get the southwest wind full on the front of the building, as it sweeps across the inner bay toward us. However by 10 P.M. the wind had died and it had stopped snowing so we were fairly comfortable during the night.

February 11, 1933 *S.W. wind, Temp. -15, 78 days*

The men started out for Crow Point but had to turn back as it was too cold. I managed to do my washing, however, and was glad I did, as the sun came out and they froze and got dried nicely.

I finished Bob's four pongee handkerchiefs which I made for his Valentines, and cut out another nightgown.

We took pictures of the frozen bay and ice-covered rocks. I hope they are good.

We listened to the Boston Symphony Orchestra in the evening — it seems truly wonderful that we, isolated on a snow-and-icebound island in Lake Superior, could be in attendance at Symphony Hall in Boston!

I have thirty-four blocks finished for my quilt and am working on my second summer nightgown.

February 12, 1933

S.W. wind,
Temp. 0, 77 days

Warmer today, and snowing generously (for a change!!) We must have six feet of snow in the woods now — I know we have plenty to plow through on the way up to the "caduvey" [Family expression for outdoor latrine].

I have my first <u>real cold</u> of the season and am eating cold-breakers and Ex-Lax religiously in order to break it up before it's a "grippy" one.

Bob is beginning to cut permanent teeth, and his first ones are loose, especially down in front. He'll soon be toothless as well as lanky and somewhat gawky. The awkward stage is about to dawn for him.

The boys found our pet duck (wild, of course) who has been swimming around here all winter, frozen to death, this morning. Poor thing! The cold spell was evidently too much for it.

We sang and played in the evening longing, oh, so much for a piano.

"The Moon was Coming over the Mountain" as we came up to bed and it is much warmer — we feel somewhat encouraged!

February 13, 1933

N. wind,
Temp. -12, 76 days

Nothing new to record today — worked hard in school and sewed in the evening.

February 14, 1933

S.W. wind,
Temp. -17, 75 days

The men didn't get home from Crow Point so we didn't have our Valentine box — as we have Valentines for everyone, we wanted to have them when everyone is here — they will probably be home tomorrow.

Heard today about the eight-day bank moratorium in Michigan — I'm beginning to wonder whether I'll have any money or not! One feels plenty helpless here in that regard!

February 15, 1933

N. wind,
Temp. -14, 74 days

Jack B. arrived from Rock Harbor just as we were having dinner, at noon — everyone is well both there, and at Tourist Home.

The men came home so we had our Valentines after supper. They were all interesting and amusing and we were quite proud of our homemade efforts!

Mr. Johnson believes we can expect the boat in about six weeks!

February 16, 1933

S. wind,
Temp. +18, 73 days

A glorious sunny day! We are hoping this nice weather will last long enough to make some impression on our heaps of snow.

Took pictures after school. Heard over the radio of the attack on President-elect Roosevelt's life which wounded Mayor Cermak and others. It was certainly brutal — makes one shudder to think of such maniacs being at large.

But — what ho! — the Senate has voted to repeal the Eighteenth Amendment! [Prohibition of alcoholic beverages.] Which should mean better times — and a decent salary for school teachers!

February 17, 1933

S.W. wind,
Temp. +18, 72 days

Here endeth the twenty-second week of school — with flying colors, as we are more than up to date in our work!

I've almost finished the blocks for my quilt — will get the rest done tomorrow.

February 18, 1933

Mr. and Mrs. Johnson set out for Rock Harbor this morning, via the snowshoe trail. They are exchanging Diamond Dyes and medicine for nails and embroidery thread. Such is high finance on Isle Royale! Bank closings bother us not — right now.

The ice is breaking up again — I'm glad — I don't like to feel so shut in. As long as the water is open, we could get out if necessary.

A fine sunny day — just right for the weekly washing of Bob and me (which I perform in a bucket) — I mean both clothes and us — and it is the same bucket, too!

February 19, 1933

Well, a February blizzard — and what a blizzard! More snow fell in two hours than we've had all winter. The folks just got back from Rock Harbor to escape the storm, which was just beginning to break into real fury as they arrived.

I sewed all day — optimistically enough — on summer underwear!

And so to bed — ten weeks to go until we are released from bondage!

February 20, 1933

S.E. storm,
Temp. 0, 69 days

The blizzard continues to rage and we are using snowshoes to go from the schoolhouse to the house. We are glad it is not so terribly cold as this schoolhouse would be anything but livable if it were 40 below — and a blizzard, to boot. It was bad enough when it was perfectly still and 40 below. The ice has all gone from the bay, but there are great drifts of snow everywhere and the trees are simply loaded with snow.

February 21, 1933

N.W. wind,
Temp. -19, 68 days

Still and very cold today. The bay is frozen over again. And is there snow! We had to shovel our way out before we could go over to breakfast. The sun came out at noon, but was not hot enough to do any damage. The men are busy mending nets preparatory to the opening of the season so it looks as if they really did expect spring sometime!

The children were out playing after school and saw a big wolf [coyote] right out on the ice near where they were playing. It ran across to the high bluff and disappeared among the trees. Wilderness indeed!

February 22, 1933

S. wind,
Temp. +40, 67 days

A wonderful spring-like day — warm and sunny. We had school in the morning. In the afternoon we came back for an hour and had stories of Washington, and some songs, and dismissed school at 2:00.

Heard tonight of a second attempt on Mr. Roosevelt's life. Someone surely does not want him to be inaugurated.

A moose slept right outside here last night — found its "bed" when we went up to the "caduvey"!

The ice is all gone again and I'm glad to hear the surf pound outside — don't feel so hemmed in!

February 23, 1933

N.W. wind,
Temp. +20, 66 days

A very dull day — everyone seemed unutterably stupid! Just one of those days!

February 24, 1933

S.W. wind,
Temp. +40, 65 days

Another warm day but strangely enough the harbor and bay are frozen over again. However the ice appears to be only a skim.

By evening the ice had completely disappeared, and we were having a heavy fall of snow, for a change! It is ten feet deep in the woods now and from five to six feet deep around the building.

February 25, 1933

S.E. wind,
Temp. +34, 64 days

Still snowing, but pleasantly warm. I've started putting my quilt blocks together now. It is to be for Bob's bed, so he helped arrange the blocks and we think it will be very pretty, with its fans and plain blue strips. He is quite proud of it and says he will take good care of his room when he has that.

We are all breaking out with ringworm — I suppose because we have so much meat and potatoes — as the vegetables are nearly all gone. Bob and I are using Lysol and Resinol externally, and Ex-Lax and plenty of water internally, but it will surely seem good to eat lettuce, and carrots, and oranges (I'd give my soul for an orange tonight!).

The family fought over the radio tonight, as usual! I can't remember our family doing that — but here they squabble continually, and the result is, we never hear anything decently. Oh, well, only nine weeks more to be endured. And so to bed — itching like the devil!

February 26, 1933

S. wind,
Temp. +40, 63 days

The lake is simply filled with pile ice today — the most they've seen in years — and where it came from is more than we know. Well, I, for one, hope the wind comes along and gets rid of it. I hate being hemmed in.

February 27, 1933

S.E. wind,
Temp. +40, 62 days

The pile ice is still with us, as far as can be seen. Mr. and Mrs. Johnson took stock of supplies today, to budget carefully as there can be no planning on an early boat now. We'll be lucky to get out by May 1, unless a miracle happens! I feel gloomy, and depressed, but still hoping!

February 28, 1933

S.E. wind,
Temp. +40, 61 days

Well, the ice is still piled outside, but it is warm and the snow is beginning to thaw.

The men returned from Crow Point — they have taken up their traps today — so winter is really approaching its end. They saw Ben and he is well, but is sure it must have been 100 below during the cold spell.

We hear Marquette WBEO today — first time! Seemed good, too, but would rather hear WHDF.

*

March 1, 1933

S. wind,
Temp. +30, 60 days

Ash Wednesday — Lent begins. I don't believe we have anything left to "give up" for Lent — we've had Lent all winter!

The ice has drifted away from outside again, thank goodness. It would surely be great to hear the "Winyah's" whistle in about three weeks.

Heard today over WBEO that there is to be boat service from Chicago to Isle Royale this year, with Marquette a port of call. That sounds encouraging to everyone here.

*

March 2, 1933

S. wind,
Temp. +40, 59 days

A beautiful spring day! Mr. Johnson and his "gang" have started their spring building — new cabins, etc. The lake is blue, and looks like the spring lake. It won't be long now.

Heard tonight of the sudden death of Senator

Walsh, Attorney General Designate. Sad to have such an event just before inauguration.

March 3, 1933

S. wind,
Temp. +50, 58 days

Another gorgeous day. The snow is thawing appreciably, and the ice, too, is departing. Hurray!

I am covered with a fierce "breaking-out" — sort of hives, I guess, which in addition to the ringworm we all have, is plenty irritating. I guess I miss oranges and tomatoes and lettuce!

Today finished the twenty-fourth week of school. Eight more to go! Mr. Johnson expects the "Winyah" anytime after the twentieth now — if the nice weather continues. I must get a letter started to Mom so as to have one ready to go when the old steamboat does arrive. And what a great day that will be!

We are all set for all the inauguration ceremonies tomorrow, with a fully-charged battery.

I took indoor flashlight pictures tonight of our "living room-workshop" — net-mending, carpet-weaving, greenstone grinding, quilt-making. No "Technocracy" on Isle Royale — we work twenty-four hours a day!

I have my quilt finished as far as I can go now, almost all my underwear made — and another two weeks will see everything finished and ready to pack!

And so to bed — aweary indeed!

March 4, 1933

N. wind,
Temp. +24, 57 days

Up early to get all work done before inauguration ceremonies began. We listened to everything and were much impressed by it all. Just as Mr. Garner was being inaugurated, Togo scared up a moose right outside the store, and we all rushed over, and out onto the dock, cameras in hand. Got some dandy shots of him, a "calf" — if only they turn out well.

We were thrilled at President Roosevelt's address — the feeling of assurance and confident leadership which he brought should do much to encourage us all.

The parade was marvelous, and for once in my life, I heard as many military bands as I wanted to hear.

The news about banks worries me still — I shall be in a nice fix if I can draw out no money! Well, in eight weeks something ought to happen! I'll surely be glad when the "Winyah" comes and I can get a letter to the bank.

It is very late now, and I'm terribly tired — after a bath in the usual "bucket" the "hay" will seem good.

So long until tomorrow!

March 5, 1933

S.W. wind,
Temp. +26, 56 days

The southwest storm piled a lot of ice outside and in our outer harbor. I wished like fury that I had had a movie camera to take a picture of it moving majestically, almost ominously toward us — like a thing inevitable, inescapable! And now we are hemmed in from the world again, with the grinding and crashing of the ice ringing in our ears constantly, maddeningly.

I believe we are all getting on each other's nerves. So many little things that other people do annoy me terribly — and yet, when I think of them in retrospect, they are such trifles — the way one person chews, the groans of another when asked to do anything, the comments on radio, politics, etc. — the children's eternal clatter! I guess confinement of the sort we have is bound to make one a bit "jittery." However, I keep still (really, believe it or not) and sew frantically to keep from exploding, although when I'm trying to listen to Rubinoff and his violin play the *Desert Song* and the rest argue over whether it is music or not, I could weep. Violet and Mrs. J. and I like music — Vivian, jazz — the kids, cowboy singers — and the men like nothing but old time fiddling and Swedish polkas. Wow!

Oh, well — this journal and Bob are my outlet. And thank goodness, it won't be too long now.

Wonder how the family all are and how soon I will hear from them!

March 6, 1933

S.W. wind,
Temp. +30, 55 days

We were extremely sorry to hear today of the death of Mayor Cermak. He surely made a game fight for his life. Mr. Roosevelt, however, does not seem to be allowing these personal griefs to lessen his activities in attempting to straighten out the country's financial mess. He seems to be right on the job!

More gray hairs today over Kenyon's reading. He surely is one stubborn child, and an enigma psychologically!

All we hear over the radio is banks, money, script!

✳

March 7, 1933

*S. wind,
Temp. +40, 54 days*

Another hectic day — Kenny is the biggest problem I have ever met in school and I am so darn discouraged. I've tried every teaching device I know, and he simply gets dumber than ever. Gosh, but I'm tired of this place — my legs just tingle with nervousness — I feel as though I'd like to just yell and yell, and get something — I don't know just what — out of my system!

Hope the boat comes this month — to bring letters and some magazines and a breath from the outside world!

March 8, 1933

N.W. gale,
Temp. +10, 53 days

Strong winds seem to have blown the cobwebs out of my system as well as all the ice out of the harbor! The men are getting everything ready to start fishing as soon as this storm dies down. The lake will be quite free of ice now and it will be safe to set out hook lines.

We hear continually of Mr. Roosevelt's "pep," and the increase of cheerfulness and confidence throughout the country. Sounds <u>good</u> to us!

March 9, 1933

N.W. gale,
Temp. -20, 52 days

What a night last night was! The wind howled while a blizzard of stinging snow raged about us and the thermometer dropped to twenty below. I was afraid to sleep on account of the shaky condition of our stovepipes and the tinderbox construction of this building, so with a hot water bottle and as many clothes as we wear outdoors ordinarily, I sat up in bed and read until my hands were nearly paralyzed with cold. Then a "warm-up" as Bob calls it — but no real sleeping. The school has been just like a barn all day, with snow seeping in through the many cracks as the blizzard continues. We managed to do our work by huddling around the stove, which simply swallows huge chunks of birch wood but refuses to give us any heat, to speak of.

We took two hours at noon, to hear the opening of the 73rd Congress. The girls are writing a "last chapter" as part of their job in American History, and we are all much interested in everything that is going on. Of course, we have to depend on the radio for all news, so must listen when programs of interest are broadcast.

Bob and I have just finished cleaning up the school and getting in a big supply of wood for tonight. We are both nearly on top of the stove — and are wearing four pair of hose each — and still Bob says, "Gee, my toes are cold!" Well, so are mine — and fingers too, so will sign off for today and hope Congress gives us a rise in temperature tomorrow.

March 10, 1933

N. wind,
Temp. +12, 51 days

Warmer today, thank goodness! The boys and Bob gave a play in the afternoon. They had asked to do it, prepared it and directed it themselves. It was a dandy! They were dressed as coons [racoons] and really were funny!

I have finished all my sewing except the tablecloth Aunt Jessie sent me, so have started that, also am sewing carpet rags to weave a rug for the Harbor house. I like running the loom, and have managed to find enough pieces to make a nice rug.

March 11, 1933

*N. wind,
Temp. +10, 50 days*

The ice in the harbor is very thick again. I walked out to the middle of the bay and took pictures and was it cold out there! It seems as though spring is a long way off!

We had to dig our wood out with ax and shovel today as it is frozen solidly together. Bob and Kenny worked away like good ones digging at it and piling some on the porch for immediate use.

March 12, 1933

*S.W. wind,
Temp. +26, 49 days*

There is so much snow and ice outside that spring looks farther away than ever. But we hope to see some signs of it before long.

Today was Junior's birthday so we had a bit of a celebration — some homemade gifts, and a cake. I sewed carpet rags all day and have a good-sized ball now.

We listened to President Roosevelt at 10 P.M. as he explained the banking situation and were much impressed by his clearcut, definite manner of speaking, as well as the <u>friendliness</u> of his voice. I expect we here on Isle Royale have been <u>least</u> affected by this banking holiday, of any one in the U.S. and yet — I don't imagine anyone has followed the development of affairs any more closely than we have!

Well, I hope Bob and I will be able to get enough money to mortgage our way home. (If and when, the "Winyah" ever succeeds in getting through the ice fields!)

*

March 13, 1933

*N.E. wind,
Temp. +30, 48 days*

No special news today. We all worked hard in school and out. Mr. Johnson has started to grind greenstones.

The ice is still solid but we are hoping this wind will break some of it up tonight.

We heard at night about the "Gold rush" of today — people bringing gold back to the banks in every imaginable container and quantity. Seems queer to us here — what is gold or money, anyway!

*

March 14, 1933

*N. wind,
Temp. +20, 47 days*

The men began to cut ice in the harbor today. The ice is gradually beginning to break up. They cut about 15,500 pounds today — expect to cut sixty tons! If the stuff holds together long enough. They usually cut about ten tons a day.

I have wrenched a muscle in my back (on the

woodpile!) and am in real misery — hobbling around like an old, old woman! (And still hauling wood — guess I'll have to die before I'm released from that job.)

Think I'll start a letter to Mom tonight to have ready when the "Winyah" gets around to coming.

✳

March 15, 1933

N. wind,
Temp. -4, 46 days

The sun shone today but it was decidedly colder and the ice is more solid than ever. We have to conserve butter and coffee now — and have to conserve kerosene even more strictly, although we've had to do that all winter!

My back gets worse instead of better — I'm hobbling about with a cane now.

✳

March 16, 1933

S. wind,
Temp. +40, 45 days

Well, today was encouraging — warm, sunny, snow melting — and a chance for legal beer soon! It does seem good to hear about better times and optimism for a change

After tomorrow just six weeks of school left! Hurray!

And my back is slightly better.

March 17, 1933

S.W. wind,
Temp. +40, 44 days

A very ordinary day — the usual Friday clean-up, etc.

I have done quite a little work on my tablecloth.

March 18, 1933

S.W. wind,
Temp. +30, 43 days

Today I had another new experience — I wove a rag rug on the big loom! And it is quite pretty if I do say so. Of course it could be a little flatter in a place or two — but for a first attempt is not so bad!

The ice is piled up outside as far as we can see, and hopes of an early boat are fast disappearing. The ice is four feet thick in the harbor, and getting thicker daily. Well — a good warm spell and some wind will send it all packing. Some of the big cakes, as they drifted majestically past here during the day shone and sparkled in the sun like huge diamonds. There was one cake which looked like a full-rigged schooner. We took a picture from the North Point — it seemed queer to be walking where water once was.

March 19, 1933

It is colder today — but we can see open water beyond the ice cakes, and there are crows building nests all around us, so Spring must be somewhere on her way.

Today, I added still another chapter to my book of new experiences — I began to grind and polish the greenstones which Bob and I found. It is fascinating work, to see the flakes of translucent, rich green appear from a dull brown stone. We have one or two nice large ones, and some clear but small stones.

March 20, 1933

The almanac says today is the first day of spring. The snow does seem to be departing, very gradually again!

The northeast wind sails the ice cakes past here toward Duluth. What we need now is warmer weather and shifting winds.

We made a "pool" today betting on when the "Winyah" will get here:

Mr. J.	April 9
Jerry	April 17
Junior	April 16
Vivian	April 2
Kenyon	April 1
Bobby	April 11

Violet	April 5
Dorothy	April 19
Mrs. J.	April 12
Uncle	April 10
Adam	April 15

(Note: Adam Roach was drowned May 2, 1933)

Well, the beer question seems to have been settled, so there should be some jobs for people soon!

March 21, 1933

S.W. wind,
Temp. +30, 40 days

Snow — snow and more snow! It has snowed steadily all day, and now at 5 o'clock is still going strong. The ice has departed from outside the harbor, going whence we know not! Spring seems farther away than ever — I feel gloomy and fidgety. Too much Isle Royale, I guess!

Kenyon's sixth birthday today, so we had games, stories and homemade presents today.

March 22, 1933

S. wind,
Temp. +50, 39 days

Well, today really seems decidedly springlike — warm, sunny, melting snow, and open water. Here's hoping we have many days like this.

I have the doors and windows wide open at 5 o'clock and am perfectly comfortable. It seems almost too good to be true.

March 23, 1933

S.W. wind,
Temp. +40, 38 days

Another spring day, with the snow melting steadily! After tomorrow, five weeks of school left. Bob and Kenny entertained us with a "delightful parade" today. They are about as graceful as a team of oxen!

March 24, 1933

S.E. wind,
Temp. -6 to +40, 37 days

From six below at 8 A.M. to forty above at noon! What weather! There are lots of birds, and the snow is melting, but the lake is piled high with ice again. Ho hum! Lazy weather, etc. — we are all getting sort of "jittery", and hoping the boat really will come in a couple of weeks.

March 25, 1933

Again the lake is frozen over — skies are gray, and it is snowing. Everyone here says it is the longest, drawn out winter they have ever had here.

We are all so tired of sewing and reading — and each other. It will be great to see a show again, have a hot bath in a tub, and read a newspaper!

✳

March 26, 1933

A gorgeously warm and sunny spring day, with the snow melting fast, and a wide strip of open water to be seen outside. We all felt so encouraged, and happy.

I finished grinding my greenstones today. Have quite a few left which are not worth grinding, but will be interesting as illustrations of how a greenstone looks before it is ground and polished. The seemingly high prices asked for these stones no longer astonishes me — it is difficult to find one large enough to grind, in the first place, and then the grinding and polishing is really a big job.

Now we are doing some birchbark work. I made a set of bridge tallies and place cards last night and I want to make napkin rings and some little photograph books for gifts. I have only one side left to do on my tablecloth — then all my sewing will be done.

March 27, 1933

S.W. wind,
Temp. +30, 34 days

Well, at last we have a west wind and the ice is gone again, thank goodness. It is not so warm today, but still the ice is melting.

March 28, 1933

N. wind,
Temp. +20, 33 days

Lake all frozen over again — not an inch of blue to be seen anywhere. Snow flurries.

March 29, 1933

S. wind,
Temp. +50, 32 days

A fine warm day — but the lake is still frozen. We look at it a hundred times a day — hoping for a change.

Mr. and Mrs. J. went to Rock Harbor today — after "snuss" [snuff].

We have the "birchbark" epidemic now and are making every conceivable object out of it.

The "jitters" still persist — and my hair has plenty of white spots, now. Oh, for a change of environment — I can hardly wait to get away now.

March 30, 1933

S.W. wind,
Temp. +40, 31 days

Today it rained hard all day, which washed away much of the dirty snow. And a heavy swell has broken up the ice in the lake, outside the harbor. In the Harbor, the ice is covered with about three inches of water.

We have been hoping to hear something about the opening of navigation over the radio, but as yet, haven't heard a thing.

However, according to Mr. Johnson's reckonings, which he says never fail, the "Winyah" will be here April 9th — just ten days from today!

March 31, 1933

N. wind,
Temp. +40, 30 days

Well, the lake is covered with ice again and the wind has gone down, but the snow continues to melt rather rapidly.

We finished our twenty-eighth week of school today — four more to go!

I have finished my tablecloth — which finishes all the sewing I have to do. I am making birchbark napkin rings, etc., now — preparing for the summer, and passing evenings away. The radio is poor now as the "B" batteries are nearly shot.

Mr. and Mrs. J. came home from Rock Harbor. They had also been down to Tourist Home. Everyone is well, but anxiously waiting for the ice to break up.

Rock Harbor Channel is frozen solid.

They had devilish walking home, as the snow is so honeycombed that snowshoes sink right to the bottom. They brought an apple a piece (from Ralph Anderson [fisherman from West Caribou Island]) and did that apple taste good. The gods may have their ambrosia! Give me an apple.

I have finished nine napkin rings — all monogrammed and varnished. Have several more cut out ready to sew. I have learned to sew them with cedar bark as the Indians do. It is much more durable than yarn. And I have learned how to <u>scrape</u> a design on certain kinds of bark. It is fun.

April 1, 1933

S. wind,
Temp. +40, 29 days

There is a wide strip of open water to be seen today. If only we'd get a good strong wind to keep the ice moving it would soon break up — but we don't seem to get any wind to amount to anything. However, Mr. J. still expects the boat a week from tomorrow.

Today we celebrated three birthdays — Mrs. J. (March 29), Violet (March 30) and Jerry (April 1) — we had homemade presents and cards and I made a cake.

The boys had a picnic out on the rocks at noon. There were many "April Fools."

We are going to have an Easter party if the boat comes so we can get some supplies. It will be a grand finale! Although we hope to have a steak roast some noon during the last week of school.

*

April 2, 1933

S. wind,
Temp. +50, 28 days

It rained all night, so the men had to dig canals around the houses as the water was seeping in all over the floors. The snow has certainly gone down a lot.

Today is warm and sunny. This morning Togo, the big collie dog, went through the ice in the middle of the Harbor, and there was a really thrilling rescue. Mr. J. pushed a ladder before him and almost inch by inch, flat on his stomach, crawled over the ice near enough to get the dog out. Then they had to edge back to shore in the same way. We have had to issue strict orders to all the children about going anywhere near the ice. It is full of airholes now.

There is open water outside today, and we see chunks of ice drifting back and forth past the entrance to the Harbor. The seagulls are doing their spring "screaming" and Mr. J. tells us to have our mail ready to go next Sunday. I'm getting quite thrilled at the prospect of the "Winyah."

April 3, 1933

N.W. wind,
Temp. +40, 27 days

We packed one box of books ready to go back to the state library, and I wrote several letters, so we are getting ready truly now. The men went out into the lake with the skiff. The ice is just thin surface ice and the strong southeast winds which the weatherman promises for tomorrow should break it up easily.

I started my birchbark basket today with Mrs. Johnson's help. It is fascinating work.

April 4, 1933

S.E. wind,
Temp. +50, 26 days

Well, the men went out in the "Pep" today and set nets. They report only isolated chunks of floating ice with open water everywhere. They had to break through ice here in the bay only.

We heard today of the sinking of the "Akron" — more disaster! And Michigan seems to have voted wet! The first state to ratify repeal of the Eighteenth Amendment!

April 5, 1933

S.E. gale,
Temp. +30, 25 days

Well, a year ago today, the "Winyah" came, but today we are having the worst storm we've had all winter.

Over three feet of new snow has fallen already, and is still coming thick and fast. Heavy seas outside have simply filled the harbor with ice. It looks worse than ever before this year. Even Mr. Johnson is discouraged. Bob and I are disgusted — we would have to strike the worst winter they've had in years — it is just in keeping with our usual bad luck. We'll probably be stuck here until June — but salary (if it can be dignified by that name) stops April 28th. Oh, hell! is all I can say. We're out of kerosene, so can't read, and almost out of gasoline, butter, coffee, canned goods. I'm sick of moose meat and potatoes! The compressed yeast is gone, and the other has soured, so we have to have sour bread, or none. No one would kick if this were February — but April! And less than two weeks till Easter!

Well, maybe I'll feel better . . .

April 6, 1933

N.W. wind,
Temp. +30, 24 days

Still snowing! At least three feet of snow fell yesterday.

The ice did break up considerably, however, which helps some.

(P.M.) Snow fell all day until we had all we could do to get back and forth over the trail.

April 7, 1933   *N.W. wind,*
                                        Temp. +40, 23 days

It has stopped snowing and the ice is well broken up. The men went out and lifted the herring nets which they had set before the snowstorm started, so we can have fresh fish for dinner tomorrow.

Mr. J. still insists the boat will leave Duluth tomorrow although it may not arrive here until Monday. Well, I, for one, hope he is right.

We have only three weeks of school left now, and most of the work is done, and well done. I feel we have made real progress in spite of our makeshift equipment.

I have made three birchbark baskets, sixteen tallies, thirty napkin rings, twelve place cards, thirty-six bookmarks and eighteen nut cups! Birchbark work is fascinating — I'd like to be able to do it as well as Mrs. Johnson does. She made me an awfully pretty birchbark <u>pocketbook</u>. Something new, in the line of pocketbooks, I'll warrant.

April 8, 1933

N.E. wind,
Temp. +50, 22 days

A lovely warm day, and the lake is blue as can be, so we really hope the "Winyah" will come tomorrow. I have ten letters ready to go, and that's about all we can send until we get some money to buy stamps.

The snow melted quite a bit during the day, but the temperature fell rapidly in the evening.

Bob got a nice <u>sunburn</u> on his face today.

April 9, 1933

N.E. wind, Full moon,
Temp. +30, 21 days

No "Winyah"! We were really quite disappointed, but I suppose we can expect her most anyday. This is the latest she's ever come to the island since she started running.

I hope we hear her whistle tomorrow. We are getting eager for news and supplies and to get our own letters started — especially to the bank!

April 10, 1933

E. wind, Rain,
Temp. +32, 20 days

It rained most all day, which should help to melt some of this huge amount of snow.

Our *Evening in Paris* programs came to an end last evening, very much to our sorrow. However, they kept up interest and suspense to the end!

I finished my six ash trays (birchbark, red lacquer and milk cans) and my birchbark match holder. Am planning to make a smoking stand — rustic by nature!

April 11, 1933

S.W. wind,
Temp. +32, 19 days

At last the wind got around to the west and blew the ice all out of the harbor, so we awoke this morning to see clear water everywhere! It was indeed a great pleasure to no longer see that awful ice all around us.

We are hoping very much that the "Winyah" will come tomorrow. The men are getting ready to fish tomorrow. Everyone is so hungry for fresh fish, and so tired of moose meat!

We listened to George Bernard Shaw tell us what "boobs" we are — and true it is, as long as we listen to <u>him</u>! I like reading his plays, but his exaggerated ego nauseates me.

April 12, 1933

S.W. wind,
Temp. +50, 18 days

A lovely day — warm and sunny. Uncle Otto brought in fresh herring for dinner and did it taste good!

While we were at dinner, I (as usual, with my eyes glued to the window which faces the lake) saw a boat passing by. We all dropped knives and forks and rushed frantically out to raise the flag for the first boat of the year. The boat did not come in — Mr. J. believes it was the Coast Guard cutter "Crawford" whose captain finds it difficult to get into Chippewa Harbor.

Now we know the "Winyah" will be here soon, as the "Crawford" usually comes first and wirelesses back ice conditions. The "Crawford" will probably anchor in Rock Harbor tonight. We hope the "Winyah" will start out tomorrow if the weather is favorable.

It certainly was thrilling to see that boat after being so isolated. My heart came up into my mouth, almost — and I felt just as one does upon arrival at a dentist's office for an extraction!

April 13, 1933

S.W. wind,
Temp. +40, 17 days

Another clear, sunny day, but none too warm.

The men went to Rock Harbor in the "Pep." The "Crawford" had been there, left again last night. They came down just to see if everyone was all right. They said the "Winyah" had been all ready to leave on the 8th, when all the ice from this way came sailing down into Duluth Harbor and closed it up as tight as a drum, so they couldn't get out. However, our strong southwest winds are clearing that out so they will probably be here Sunday.

It seems good to hear something from the outside world even though the "Crawford's" crew reported times to be harder than ever (which is decidedly contrary to all we've been hearing over the radio!)

Anyway, I haven't given up hope and prefer to be optimistic as long as I possibly can be.

Bob brought me a bunch of pussy willows today — the first of the season!

April 14, 1933

S.W. wind,
Temp. +40, 16 days

Still blowing strong from the southwest, so Duluth Harbor ought to be getting cleared out and we hope the boat will be here Sunday.

Today being Good Friday, I gave the children half-a-day off and spent the afternoon cleaning the schoolhouse and packing the traveling library — ready for its return trip to Lansing.

The gulls are screaming so today that I'm about ready to scream with them. I wonder why they start that as soon as the weather begins to get the least bit warm?

We heard today that Huey P. Long has been removed from the Senate. I think it's about time. We were all glad to hear that they've started a bit of spring house-cleaning, even in the <u>august Senate</u>.

I cut out more birch work baskets for Gret and a smoking set for Jim for their birthdays.

✻

April 15, 1933

N.W. wind,
Temp. +50, 15 days

Well the season's big day is over! The "Winyah" has been here! We were all busily working when we heard her whistle down at Wright's Island. We had an hour to finish up our work and spruce ourselves up a bit. When she whistled at the Harbor entrance, I felt just like crying, and was so nervous I just shook — felt much worse than I did when she left!

We had letters from the family and the news was all encouraging. They are all well — and working some — so it isn't as bad as it might be.

We loaded up with supplies and ordered a case of beer. The "Winyah" crew was the same as ever — and old Martin hid a real interest and pleasure in our welfare, beneath his usual crustiness!

The "Winyah" needs a coat of paint badly — but she looked like the "Berengaria," "Majestic" and the Vanderbilt yacht all rolled into one — to us!

And now, the winter is truly over — our exile ended. It has been fun in many respects and I believe I could tackle it another year if nothing else turns up. Well, we will see. I'll keep the journal until we hit Duluth, and then write *finis* to the "Big Adventure."

April 16, 1933

S. wind,
Temp. +60, 14 days

A glorious Easter day — warm and sunny! The snow melted like the proverbial snowball in — well, for convention's sake, I suppose we must say, the lower regions.

Worked all day wrapping books, checking supplies and making out a requisition for next year.

April 17, 1933

S.W. wind,
Temp. +60, 13 days

Another glorious spring day, playing havoc with our heaps of snow! The air is just grand!

The men are fishing now so we all get up early, and I got half-a-dozen letters written before school.

We were through early today and did some work outside. There are a dozen miniature Niagaras rushing down to the lake, and our huge ash pile just is <u>not</u> anymore.

I wrote ten more letters after school. Will soon be caught up on all correspondence again.

Am out of stationery now.

April 18, 1933

N.W. wind,
Temp. +70, 12 days

More nice weather to record for which let us be duly thankful!

They aren't getting many fish these days, though — only six trout on a whole flock of hooklines yesterday. (Last year they got seven hundred pounds on the same amount of lines!)

The "Winyah" surprised us all by coming today at 2:00. Brought Bob and me a nice package from the Lane's in Florida — no letters at all! But we mailed sixteen — also two boxes to Alice, and the traveling library.

It was a gorgeous day and we had our afternoon classes out on the porch.

After school we varnished our birchbark work and found that we had quite a big collection of baskets, smoking sets, etc.

The men went to Rock Harbor for the night so we had toasted cheese and onion sandwiches for supper, and sewed and listened to the radio in peace!

April 19, 1933

N.E. wind,
Temp. +70, 11 days

More lovely weather — it seems almost too good to last! The snow is practically all gone now.

Finished the smoking sets yesterday — now they only need varnish.

And we seem to be off the Gold Standard.

April 20, 1933

N.E. wind,
Temp. +70, 10 days

More nice weather — and mud! But we don't mind that as long as the snow is going so fast.

We heard Canadian steamers all day. Also heard a boat going toward Wright's Island — may have been the Conservation officers.

We are working on the photograph album for George Burgan now; making it entirely of birchbark.

April 21, 1933

N. wind,
Temp. +40, 9 days

Much colder today, but the sun is still shining.

The "Winyah" came at 10:30 — she couldn't get into Duluth harbor last time up but had to lay over at Two Harbors.

Our three letters all were full of bad news — Alice tells us that the Copper Country is in a very bad way, Maria and Annie wrote that Grossmama has been very ill and has to be very careful — and the bank, sending me less than half the money I asked for on account of "restrictions" — well, how I'm going to manage to pay our winter expenses is beyond me! I'll just have to divide up what I did get and pay the rest as it is released by the bank. I was so upset by the mail that I went all to pieces. After putting in a winter in this lonely spot and working hard for that measly $65 — then not to be able to use it! And we need clothes and traveling money!

I'm going to hunt for a job as soon as I get to Chicago, believe me.

I hope the "Winyah" brings better news next time!

*

April 22, 1933

N.E. wind, Temp. +40, 8 days

Worked hard all day cleaning clothes, pressing and packing. We all went to bed early, hoping it wasn't going to be too awfully cold!

*

April 23, 1933

S.W. wind, Temp. +50, 7 days

Got up early to listen to the *Children's Hour* program over the NBC.

Ben Benson arrived about noon on his first trip of the year. He spent the winter, all alone except for two cats, on Malone Island, an island in one of the bays south of here. He is well, but found the winter plenty long — and very cold! Says he is sure it was 100 below in February.

We learn that another fish boat from Duluth is to make one trip a week, which the fishermen hope will boost the price of fish a little.

Finished all my birchbark work today, so I can pack the box and send it this week.

✳

April 24, 1933
N. wind, Rain,
Temp. +50, 6 days

Lake so rough that the men couldn't get out to their hook lines.

The "Winyah" came at 11:00. Mom has bought a ticket for us — Duluth to Chicago by bus — special rates, which will save us some money. Hope we'll be able to leave early enough on Sunday to get to Duluth in time for the bus Monday. We will leave all shopping until Chicago is reached. Sig expects to go to Chicago too, so we all ought to have fun. I'm getting eager to leave now.

Mr. Johnson went up to Duluth to sell his furs today. Hope they get a good price for them as fish is down to eight cents a pound and they are so discouraged.

The "Amaranth" passed here at noon, headed toward Passage Island Light.

April 25, 1933

N. wind,
Temp. +24, 5 days

What a <u>cold</u> morning this was! I made a fire at 6 A.M. — but it didn't get really warm in school until noon.

The children cleaned books and packed them away this morning. We start exams on Thursday.

Packed the big box of birch work and boats and moose horns. Hope it gets to Chicago without mishap.

April 26, 1933

N.W. wind,
Temp. +30, 4 days

Another cold day! I had hoped to be able to send some flowers to the folks but with this cold weather, there just aren't <u>any</u> flowers!

We finished all our work today — notebooks, book cleaning, packing of supplies into boxes — and all are ready for our two days of exams. It scarcely seems possible that the school year is really so nearly over. The time has really passed very quickly everything being considered.

April 27, 1933

S.W. wind,
Temp. +70, 3 days

A fine warm day. We began exams today, and managed to get most of the morning work done, before the "Winyah" arrived to disrupt our peace and quiet!

Old Sibilsky says he cannot promise a school for the island next year, as funds may be insufficient. Well, the Johnsons will be right on his coat tail this summer!

I ordered ice cream for a treat for the kids today, so we had enough for noon and evening meals.

Finished exams early in afternoon, so I got papers all checked and marks recorded. It simply does not seem possible that our time is so short now!

Mrs. Mac sent me the clipping from Manthei Howe's column about us. Nice!

The fishermen are disgusted because Martin is paying only seven cents a pound for trout, and it is retailing in Duluth for eighteen to twenty cents per pound! He needs competition!

April 28, 1933

N. wind,
Temp. +40, 2 days

We woke this morning to find the ground covered with snow again! But the sun came out and we soon had slush and now it is just on the verge of snowing again.

Well, school is all over now! Finished the exams in the morning and marked cards, reports, etc., in the afternoon, as well as packing supplies and giving the school a last good cleaning, washing curtains, etc. It really doesn't seem possible that the eight months are gone. On the whole it has been a pleasant, and I think, successful adventure. I sort of hate to leave now — I always hate to leave after I've become attached to a place. Schoolteachers are like sailors — always on the move!

We hear from Nan B. that WHDF is to open Monday which is good news indeed! Sorry we won't be here to listen in.

Heard a good interview with President Roosevelt's secretary on Edwin C. Hill's *Friday* program.

April 29, 1933

S.W. wind,
Temp. +50, 1 day

Well, this is the last entry I'll make on Isle Royale — for this time, at least. Will finish up this journal tomorrow, I guess — although I may decide to keep it until we get to Chicago.

We were busy today washing, ironing and finishing our packing. I see where I'll have to send several dresses to the cleaner, for our smoky stove did its work even though they were in a clothes bag.

The schoolhouse looks so queer and bare, with the pictures down, curtains also, and books all stowed away. I hate to see it and am glad we are leaving. But

I surely hope the youngsters have a school next year!

*

April 30, 1933 *N.E. gale, Much rain*

No boat today — we sat and waited. Big sea outside.

*

May 1, 1933 *Still N.E. and Rain*

Again — no boat. Still waiting.

*

May 2, 1933 *N. wind, Sunny*

"Winyah" came at 11 A.M. and we left for Duluth. Trip up pleasant, but rough — we were OK though.

*

May 3, 1933

Arrived Duluth 6 A.M.

How To Grind Greenstones

Materials necessary:
Greenstones
sealing-wax
small sticks
low pan, water, cloth
matches
carborundum powder
silver polish
grindstone with 5 wheels

Choose a greenstone which looks as if it would be clear. Shape it roughly on a coarse wheel, then make the bottom of the stone perfectly flat. Place the stone on a stick with sealing-wax, then trim down the stick. Now perfect the shape, and grind out flaws on a fine wheel. Then dip the stone into water, carborundum powder, and polish on the wet wooden wheel until smooth and glossy.

Then wet the felt wheel, and spread with silver polish; dip the stone into the polish, and put on the wheel, until the wheel is dry. Finish the polish by placing the stone on the soft wheel, until it is clean and shining.

Editor's Note: Greenstones are pebble sized, semi-precious stones that dot some of the Island's beaches. To scientists they are "chlorastrolite" (green-star-stone). In 1973, greenstone was chosen as the Michigan state gem.

Epilogue

Having momentous thoughts that some day this journal may be published and become part of the recorded history and lore of Isle Royale, it did not seem right to have this adventure come to such an abrupt ending as the final two or three entries would indicate. In fact Isle Royale was, and continues to be, a very important part of our family chronicles.

Remember, in that period of time, the Island was truly remote and inaccessible. There was no running down to the corner grocery store for more food or to the hardware for a fresh battery. There wasn't a doctor readily available, communication was at a minimum, and transportation to the mainland was almost impossible. One (even a youngster six years old) cannot go through a year of isolation, hardship, adventure, fun, wonderful companionship, and other feelings that beg description, without many unique characteristics being developed. If every one on this good old earth could have a similar winter on Isle Royale, I have a feeling that the world would be a much better place.

Now, standing on the Brockway Mountain Drive and looking across our beloved Lake Superior at the low, gray silhouette of Isle Royale, it is hard to imagine how one, long ago, winter could have been so hard, yet so rewarding.

After we arrived at Duluth, we immediately

embarked for Chicago and the Century of Progress World Fair. What a change from our winter of isolation! Then an overnight trip on the Milwaukee Road's Copper Country Limited to Calumet — dining car, pullman and all. Talk about a change in perspective!

My mother (Dot) always talked about going back to the Island, but somehow she never made it. It was always in her thoughts though, and she promoted Isle Royale with anyone she ever met. We continued to reminisce every time we were together, right up to her passing away on June 27, 1984.

I was fortunate enough to be able to go back to Chippewa Harbor several times. Mr. Johnson acquired a small excursion boat, the "Aw-wa-neesha" and ferried passengers from Eagle Harbor to his resort on the Island. I was always welcome to go along and spend some time visiting with my good friend Kenyon.

The Holger Johnson family had one addition after we left the Island, a little girl, Nancy. When Isle Royale became a National Park, the Johnsons moved to Eagle Harbor. Since that time both Holger and his wife, Lucy, have passed away. Violet married and is Mrs. Miller, living in Ahmeek, Michigan. I run into her at arts and craft shows where she demonstrates the skills she learned on the Island. Holger, Jr. married and also lives locally — in Kearsarge.

My mother remarried in 1946 and became Dorothy Simonson McQuown. I also was married in 1946 — to Jean Brown, a Calumet native. We live in my mother's home in Stambaugh, Michigan in the winter and have a summer home at Agate Harbor. My wife and I and two sons have made one trip to Isle Royale and hope to make a couple more — knowing that things never stay the same, but hoping to catch some of the sense of that exciting winter of many years ago.

Bob Simonson
February 20, 1988

Holger Johnson family: back row, left to right: Otto Olson (Holger's cousin), Vivian, Gerald (Jerry), Violet, Holger, Lucy (Mrs. Johnson). Front row, left to right: Kenyon (Kenny) and Holger Jr. and Togo their dog.

--- Violet Johnson Miller Photo Collection — early 1930's